HERE ON GILLIGAN'S ISLE

(PHOTO BY GABI RONA)

HERE ON GILLIGAN'S ISLE

by **RUSSELL JOHNSON**

with **STEVE COX**

HarperPerennial

A Division of HarperCollins*Publishers*

FIRST EDITION

Designed by Irving Perkins Associates

Library of Congress Cataloging-in-Publication Data
Johnson, Russell.
Here on Gilligan's Isle / Russell Johnson, Steve Cox.—1st ed.
p.   cm.
ISBN 0-06-096993-8 (pbk.)
1. Gilligan's Island (Television program) 2. Johnson, Russell. I. Cox, Stephen,
1966–   . II. Title.
PN1992.77.G53J64   1993
791.45'72—dc20   92-54847

93 94 95 96 97 PS/RRD 10 9 8 7 6 5 4 3 2 1

This is for David and Kimberly,
for Courtney and Max
. . . and for the "child" in everyone
R.J.

Cheers to the Skipper—Alan Hale,
who bought me a beer at his
restaurant when I was just sixteen
S.C.

CONTENTS

MAHALO!
(That's Hawaiian for
"thank you")

〜〜〜〜〜〜〜〜〜〜〜〜〜〜〜〜

THE authors are grateful to the following individuals for their contributions to this book: Jefrey Abraham, Henny Backus, Terry Bales, Ken Beck, Tom Brown, Bruce Button, Ramona Christophel, Gerald and Blanche Cox, Darren Dill, Jeff Forrester, Tom Forrester, Mark Gilman, Joey Green, Naomi "Trinket" Hale, Rosemary Hutton, Kirby Johnson, Sammy Keith, Stephen Kelley, Kevin Marhanka, Nell McCormick, Matthew Mead (at TBS), Scott Michaels, Tim Neeley, Park College (David Crowell, John Lofflin, Norm Robertson, Les Bradley, Mark Kulda), George Patterson, Bob Rankin (of the original Gilligan's Island Fan Club, Salt Lake City), Joel Rasmussen, Gino Salomone, Darlene Schwartz, Vito Scotti, Ross Shafer, Tom Shales, Ed Wade, Joe Wallison, Dave Woodman.

A round of applause to our editor, Jennifer Hull, and fellow Castaways (in order of the theme song): Bob Denver, Alan Hale, Jim Backus, Natalie Schafer, Tina Louise, and Dawn Wells. And to my wonderful wife, Connie, who lives on an island with me, and is amused by the Professor.

Photo Acknowledgments: If it weren't for my brother, Kenneth, who salvaged many photographs from my career, this book would be incomplete. For additional illustrations I wish to acknowledge CBS Television; Sherwood Schwartz; photographer Gabor Rona; *TV Guide*®; and Personality Photos, Inc./Howard Frank Archives (P.O. Box 50, Midwood Station, Brooklyn, N.Y. 11230).

Uncut, remastered videotapes of "Gilligan's Island" are available by subscription from Columbia House. For information, call 800-457-0866.

FOREWORD
by Sherwood Schwartz,
creator-writer-producer
of "Gilligan's Island"

I T'S easy to underestimate the importance of the Professor on "Gilligan's Island." Was he as funny as Gilligan and the Skipper? Of course not. Was he as witty as Mr. and Mrs. Howell? Heavens to Wall Street, no. Was he as sexy as Ginger or as cute as Mary Ann? Are you kidding? Then why was he so important?

Because it was the Professor who held the whole show together. He was the cement that kept those odd-shaped bricks in place. Without him, the characters on the island would have collapsed. His lone voice of reason was invariably the one that prevailed above the cacophonous chorus of the other Castaways.

Most actors who play earnest and logical characters become dull and boring. But Russell Johnson turned earnest and logical into an amusing art form. He spoke complicated phrases and complex formulas with such eloquence that he made them sound completely believable. In the process, he turned the Professor into a character just as unforgettable as the other Castaways. The Professor on "Gilligan's Island" became the academic icon of the television age.

The Professor's influence can best be illustrated by a learning test used on an educational channel in Philadelphia. A class was shown film clips of the Professor's experiments in various episodes of "Gilligan's Island": the way he recharged the radio batteries by

This is one of the last portraits of us taken as a group. We're with Sherwood Schwartz, posing behind our voodoo doll likenesses that were used in "Voodoo." (© 1988 BY TAMMY LECHNER)

using different metals and seawater, the way he made glue from sap, glass from sand, and so forth. Another class was taught the same information by a regular teacher. The students learned the information four times as well from the Professor. That's because Russell Johnson, as an actor, made that information unforgettable. Besides, the Professor was more than a teacher to the students. He was a friend.

When the series started, Russell and I had a long talk. He needed my reassurance that he wasn't merely spouting gibberish when he used the scientific terminology. He needed to believe what he was saying in order to be convincing. I promised him that it would make sense. The equations might not balance properly, and the experiments might not achieve the precise result, but we would always use actual elements from the periodic table and respect their properties. Russell never had a problem after that, and he rattled off the technical jargon with clarity and precision. Sometimes, when it seemed to me that some of the words at the script's first reading were jawbreakers, I offered to make changes so they would be easier to say. Russell would always reply, "I'm an actor. It's my job to speak the words as written." And he did.

In fact, one day, as a practical joke, I wrote a phony speech for the Professor that wasn't really intended to be used in the show. I loaded it with so much technical polysyllabic verbiage that it had no meaning, and the combination of letters rendered it unfit for human pronunciation. I thought we'd have a laugh the next day at the reading when Russell tried to say it aloud. Instead, Russell pronounced that entire half page of meaningless words absolutely without flaw. Every single syllable. Not only that, he spoke with complete authority. The laugh was on me. Russell suspected my intentions and had worked on the speech half the night just to prove to me he could say anything that was written.

You see, contrary to the serious, thoughtful Professor, Russell has a wonderful sense of humor. He was a delight to work with on the series and in the many reincarnations "Gilligan's Island" enjoyed, all the made-for-television films as well as both animated series. I have the greatest admiration and affection for the Professor and the greatest admiration and affection for Russell Johnson as well.

Sherwood Schwartz

AN UNNECESSARY INTRODUCTION

~~~~~~~~~~~~~~~~~~~~~~~~~~~~~~~~~~~

GILLIGAN: Hiya, Professor. What are you doing?
PROFESSOR: I'm making notes for a book. It's to be a chronicle of our adventures on the island . . . I think it's a book people will buy, don't you?
GILLIGAN: Sure, I'll buy one. I'm dying to find out what happens to us.

—EPISODE #2, "HOME SWEET HUT"

It's time for this book.

In the mid-1960s I was stuck somewhere in the South Pacific with six others, swimming through network ratings, and problems, and friendships, and family. Nearly thirty years have passed since the seven of us signed those unfortunate contracts and landed on "Gilligan's Island." That series has affected my life every day since. In fact, today I live with my wife on an island. Old habits die hard.

At this point, it's doubtful there is much could I say that would sour the appeal of "Gilligan's Island," even though there have been many times I have refused to reveal aspects of my relationships with these fellow Castaways, these friends of mine. So you may find a few surprises.

It's a tough, strong, funny little show, this "Gilligan's Island," and it just won't go away. And now we have a President who watched "Gilligan's Island" growing up, right along with the rest of the baby boomers.

Especially to those who watched the show when they were children and grew up with us in reruns, I *am* the Professor, just as Bob Denver *is* Gilligan. This is the power of television.

Every day I encounter fans who approach me, sometimes nervously, sometimes so casually you would think we were on the island together. "Hey, aren't you the . . .?" There are some who have seen the episodes so many times they can tell you which one is which from the opening shot: "Oh, this is the one where Gilligan sees everything upside down!"

And I must say, it's flattering when science-fiction buffs remember some of the fifties flicks I did when 3-D was starting to get warm, like *It Came From Outer Space.* At least sometimes somebody recalls me in something *other* than "Gilligan's"! I guess I'm finally resigned to the Professor being my most famous role, my claim to fame. Funny how these things work out.

Still, the fallout from this island haunts me, although it stopped plaguing me to the point of misery a while back. Since "Gilligan's Island," my life has hit highs and lows. A few years after my first wife Kay passed away, I married Constance Dane. Connie was an actress in many television shows, among them "The George Burns and Gracie Allen Show," "Father Knows Best," "Matinee Theatre," and "Tallahassee Seven Thousand."

Connie is beautiful, spiritual, and she's my "manager." Her advice is invaluable, especially regarding this book, and I love her dearly.

So here's the Professor and his wife living on an inhabited island in Puget Sound in a beautiful home surrounded by a wooded heaven, where deer come right up to our patio door. Above the mantel is a gift from Sherwood Schwartz: a masterfully matted-and-framed portrait in glorious color of the seven stranded castaways, hanging directly over the fireplace.

Believe it or not, until recently the idea of being on an island never held much appeal for me. As a bombardier in World War II, I was shot down over one, and in the 1960s my career got stranded on one. "Gilligan's Island" has been "a mixed blessing" in every sense of the cliché. Sure, it gave me fame and recognition long after it should have died a natural death. But I'll warn you: There was a time when I was not at all proud of being one of a seven-man totem pole, one of "the rest," on a show that was universally proclaimed by the critics to be crap.

Twice I turned down invitations to test for the series. Finally, when I gave in, I took on the role of the Professor simply for the compensation. All I knew was that it was a job that helped me support my family. What I told *TV Guide* back in the sixties still applies: "It's cold out, boy. It's rough. If you're an actor, you should work as an actor."

In the beginning, both Tina Louise and I stood under the same dark cloud of apprehension about doing this show, maybe more so than the others. Come to think of it, Natalie Schafer—you know, Mrs. Howell—was noticeably disappointed that the show was actually purchased and set to start. Natalie had lived in New York for a long time, and she was most comfortable there. She accepted the role for the pilot just to cash in on a free trip to Hawaii. She thought the script was "dreadful." It never entered her mind that anybody would actually *like* the show.

As for me, I felt mighty overqualified, and it really disturbed me. For years I was trained in the theater, and I was always serious about what I did as an actor. Tina was a bit more forceful when she blurted publicly that she was "ashamed" of the show—while we were still filming new episodes each week.

Still, every one of us always pulled it off for the camera. In the final analysis, that's all that matters. We took the job seriously, and regardless of any problems with each other or difficulties at home, we worked closely together and made the best of it. I'm convinced that our creator, Sherwood Schwartz, couldn't have hired better people. I'm not afraid to brag a bit. My work is good. I'm a damn good actor, and that's equally true of the six others in the cast.

In just three seasons on CBS we created almost a hundred episodes—that's equivalent to the output of five seasons now. I was always happy to be working with such competent, talented actors, but silently my displeasure rose after we were canceled and the show plagued me. I didn't realize it at first, but because of "Gilligan's," I was going to have a difficult time reestablishing a career.

Then a funny thing happened. Over the years I began noticing something unusual about "Gilligan's Island." I looked at what television kept producing. And you know what? I realized we really weren't so bad after all. The show's uniqueness became apparent. I never imagined the show would maintain such a warm appeal ten, twenty, or even thirty years later.

Everyone keeps telling me that "Gilligan's" is "a cult hit show," whatever that means. I suspect it indicates longevity, a strong appeal, and a loyalty toward a show that was instilled in many viewers' lives during their childhoods. It's true that people develop strange and lasting feelings for whatever TV shows they devoured when they were growing up. Here, three decades later, I still get recognized by fans who loved the show and *know* those characters and episodes.

For a few of us, our characters weren't far from our real personalities. I can say the Professor was (and is) a part of me, but I also left him at the studio when I came home at night. Alan Hale, on the other hand, kept a sort of camaraderie with his alter ego. He loved the character, and Alan really *became* the Skipper and rarely left his house without that cap. Natalie Schafer—she was the very same as Mrs. Howell, only kinder. I don't think Tina Louise ever really embraced Ginger Grant.

None of us thought the show would last. Some of us thought it wouldn't last a full season. I certainly never thought we were doing work that would someday, years down the line, be dissected by fans. None of us had that idea, except maybe Sherwood Schwartz—and I think he's the only one still collecting paychecks from the show. We had no idea we would become so much a part of the public's consciousness, so why save mementos? Why sock away the scripts?

And so there are a handful of "Gilligan's Island" episodes that I catch today, and I sit there astounded. I have absolutely no recollection of ever performing in some of them. The memory of them is gone. Wiped.

Here's where a young guy by the name of Steve Cox comes in. Steve and I met in 1986 while I was doing a play in Kansas City, Missouri. He invited me to what he described would be a "tribute to 'Gilligan's Island' " at his college, so I went. No pay. It was just for the hell of it. I thought, "This is gonna be either really-nice or really-awful." It turned out really nice.

I signed autographs for some very beautiful coeds, ate a terrific Chinese lunch with Steve and his friends, and then greeted a theater full of students and faculty who waited to meet this gray-haired actor. I got a kick out of the posters around Parkville's Park College. Under my face it read: "See a *real* Professor speak." It was an impromptu kind of thing, and they showed an episode of "Gilligan's" on the big screen. Huge. The school's department head even appointed me Honorary Professor of Communication Arts. That afternoon did my heart good.

After that, Steve put his journalism degree to use and began researching a book of his own about "Gilligan's," and, with tenacity, he met with all seven of us, including Tina Louise, which was no easy task. She rarely makes herself accessible when it comes to the "dreaded" island.

Steve and I kept in touch, and he even visited the set of "ALF," when four of us Castaways put on our island costumes and appeared

UNBEKNOWNEST TO THE OTHERS ON THE ISLAND, "THE PROFESSOR" KEPT A SECRET DIARY.

in a dream sequence with the furry alien rodent. Eventually, his book was, well, "marooned," so recently we decided to combine notes and provide you with the complete history of the longest three-hour tour in the history of television.

So, I'm not going to formally introduce each of the actors because you're just going to call us the Professor or Mary Ann anyway. That's all right—as long as you understand that this book is how *I* perceived "Gilligan's Island." This story is from my hut, looking out.

I'm an actor, and although this may not be the scholarly dissertation you were expecting from the island egghead, I do try to take a logical and practical stance, as the Professor would.

This book will tell you how "Gilligan's Island" hit the charts and how it nearly capsized careers. So just sit right back . . .

ANOTHER ISLAND

W HE N I flew as an Army Air Corps bombardier-navigator in World War II, I was shot down in the Philippines over a town called Zamboanga. In fact, there's an old song that goes back to the forties called "The Monkeys Have No Tails in Zamboanga." I don't know who wrote it, where it came from, or who may have recorded it, but it exists.

I joined the army on my eighteenth birthday, because it was the patriotic thing to do. Now I'm not trying to feed you a story of nobility or nationalism. It's just that the United States was noticeably more unified then. When I graduated from high school, I couldn't wait to get into the thick of combat. Since I had had military training at school, I thought, "If I'm gonna do this, I'm gonna become an officer," and I set out to do that.

It was the fourth of March 1945, about nine o'clock in the morning. I was on my forty-fourth mission, firing a .50 caliber machine gun from one of three B-25s that would be shot down that day.

We were flying at minimum altitude, or "on the deck," which means about fifty feet above the water. We were skip-bombing and strafing. The pilot was firing fourteen forward-fire, .50 caliber machine guns by pressing just one button on his controls. With another button he dropped four 500-pound bombs, which skipped across the water like flat rocks across a lake.

This was my official identification during the war. So now you know my age.
(AUTHOR'S COLLECTION)

This is how we were shot down: The Japanese blasted twenty- and forty-millimeter guns that set both of our plane's engines on fire. We knew we were going to have to ditch the plane in the water, so we went into automatic and quickly began the routine we had to go through in order to do so. The first order was to get rid of everything loose, then brace yourself with your back to the front of the airplane.

The plane would hit twice. If you have any control at all, you keep your nose up, and your tail hits first. It's the second hit that's deadly. It's like hitting a brick wall at a hundred miles an hour. If you haven't disposed of the machine guns, or anything else loose, they can smash into you with enough velocity to kill you instantly.

We took a direct hit while the engines were on fire. We were in the rear of the airplane, in the radio compartment. The shell sprayed shrapnel into me and broke my ankles. It killed the radio operator next to me. He was only on his eighth mission.

Our crew was picked up by the Army Air–Sea Rescue Service, which flew flying boats called PBYs. The army had some jet-black PBYs assigned to them, and we called them Black Cats. They circled at a set of map coordinates generally a hundred miles from where the air strike was taking place. We were in a strait of water just a couple of miles wide, between Zamboanga and an island called Basilan. We could see the Japanese were coming out after us in boats. Each of our life rafts carried six guys. With life-saving efficiency, the rest of our group of forty-eight airplanes saw the Japanese, formed a line, and strafed, sinking the Japanese boats before they could get to us.

We had radioed "Mayday." After an hour in the water, we could see the Black Cat, which landed nearby to take us aboard. We began to taxi on the water, attempting to take off, but the Black Cat was too heavy. The crew had to throw equipment overboard, and we then made it off the water and back to our base on the Halmahera Islands, which had a small station hospital.

The medic stop was a transfer point for any seriously injured soldiers. They shipped me to a New Guinea general hospital, where I occupied a bed among rows in the officers' ward. It was a tent structure like the one on "M*A*S*H," only our floors were coral, which was tough on your feet. There were guys lying on cots who had really been shot up.

I earned my Purple Heart from that mission. I remember I was lying down when I was awarded the medal. Two men came up to my bed, one carrying a stack of black boxes. The officer read the routine orders with no emotion at all: "For wounds received in action . . . Second Lieutenant Russell Johnson, 0765497, is hereby awarded the Purple Heart by order of Colonel Smith." Or *some* colonel.

When the officer finished his speech, the sergeant with him put a little spin on the box as he tossed it at me. It slid across my chest and stopped at my throat. It was an interesting way to be awarded the Purple Heart. Later on, I was also awarded the Air Medal with Oak Leaf cluster, the Asiatic-Pacific Theater of War ribbon with four battle stars, and the Philippean Liberation medal. I'm proud of my career in the military. I was in the service for three years and ten days and was honorably discharged with the rank of First Lieutenant on November 22, 1945.

Immediately thereafter, the GI Bill allowed me to enroll in the Actors Lab in Hollywood and my career as an actor began.

THE ACTORS
LABORATORY

J U S T after World War II, I started attending classes at the Actors
Lab in Hollywood on January 2, 1946.

Acting was what I had wanted to do since high school. I knew I
was good at it, so through the GI Bill, I was in the first class of GIs to
attend this prestigious theater school, which stemmed from the old
Actors Studio in New York. The Actors Studio was a powerful entity
on the East Coast, well respected in the theater world. And out of it
came the Actors Lab in Hollywood.

In a two-year program, we were taught the Stanislavski method by
talented actor-teachers, among whom were Morris Carnovsky, Sam
Levene, Hume Cronyn, Jessica Tandy, and Anthony Quinn. Kon-
stantin Stanislavski taught acting in the 1920s, introducing a "realis-
tic" approach. Without getting too technical in my explanation, it
provided you, as an actor, with a way to investigate, work out, and
perform a character in a play, night after night, from the inside out.
Not the outside in.

The Actors Lab became my "university." I attended classes from
9:00 A.M. to noon and from 1:00 P.M. until 4:00 P.M. At night we
attended plays, films, critiques, lectures, and sometimes additional
courses. Eventually, for me it became a twenty-four-hour labor of
love. I not only studied acting, but learned fencing, body movement,

voice and speech, dancing, history of the theater, set construction, and other aspects of theater.

The Actors Lab rapidly became known in Hollywood as *the* place to learn the craft. Everybody in the business came to see our plays, and it ended up being a terrific entrée into casting offices and a way to make contacts with producers of both plays and motion pictures. Marilyn Monroe studied there. She had been sent by 20th Century-Fox to hone her skills long before she became known in films— years before *The Asphalt Jungle*.

Although it wasn't until about four years later that I made my film debut, in the ensuing years I worked at the B. B. Pen company constructing ballpoint pens, I drove a cab, and I prepared cars for a dealership's showroom. I married a beautiful actress and writer named Kay Levy, who went by the professional name of Kay Cousins. Then my break came when actor-producer Paul Henreid helped me get started by putting me in a film called *For Men Only*. Paul, you'll recall, was the actor opposite Bette Davis in the classic 1942 film *Now Voyager* who lit two cigarettes at once and handed Miss Davis one. Paul also played Ingrid Bergman's husband in *Casablanca*.

For Men Only was my big break. It was a film about hazing in fraternities, and I played a heavy—you know, the villain. I love playing heavies, and this was the first of many such roles for me— until "Gilligan's Island," of course. I am one of many actors who have to credit Paul Henreid, a generous man who is now gone, for a start in films. Somebody from Universal Studios saw the picture, and eventually several of us in the film were signed to contracts as studio players.

I also have to credit Paul for one of my most embarrassing moments. He and his wife had invited my wife Kay and me to his home for dinner one evening. We knew there were going to be other people there, and Kay and I ran around like crazy attempting to make the dinner on time. For some reason, things kept going wrong and we knew we were going to be late. When we finally started out, the front door jammed and wouldn't open. The whole door was stuck shut. I ended up having to remove the door from its hinges so we could leave. When we got to the party, everyone was waiting for us. And

For Men Only (1952) was my first film. It was about fraternity hazing and was directed by and starred Paul Henreid (on right), who gave me my first big chance in the business. (AUTHOR'S COLLECTION)

there, sitting at the head of the long table, was the evening's guest of honor: Charlie Chaplin.

Meeting the gray-haired Chaplin was nothing less than an honor and a privilege. Mr. Chaplin held court. When he talked, everyone stopped eating and sipping and just listened.

Outside of some Westerns I made at Universal, I ended up doing some science-fiction flicks in which I played scientists, precursors to the Professor, I guess. They turned out to be cult movies, like *It Came from Outer Space*, one of the first films made in 3-D.

That film took a lot of energy because we shot it twice, once with the 3-D camera, which was manufactured right there at Universal, and again with the regular 2-D camera technique. The same year I made the science-fiction film *This Island Earth*, where I played a regular guy, scientist Steve Carlson, who gave his life to save the others. Jack Arnold, who later ended up directing most of the "Gilligan's" episodes, directed the film. He also directed *Space Children*, a film I did at Paramount, of which I have absolutely no recollection. I know it's on my résumé and fans quiz me about it, but for some reason it's like I have amnesia about that one, which might be best.

A lot of sci-fi fans ask me about another "classic," *Attack of the Crab Monsters*, which is so bad it's good. *Crab Monsters* was a 1957 drive-in favorite directed by Roger Corman, who made a reputation in Hollywood for producing films quickly and with very little money.

Corman was a no-nonsense guy. There was no sitting down and discussing what was really going on in a scene between the characters. No time for that. The only direction he gave was "You gotta get out of the way of these crabs 'cause they're gonna kill you!" That was it.

I remember in *Crab Monsters* I broke my toe in a scene in which I had to come up out of the ocean wearing some scuba gear along with the girl in the picture. We were supposed to shoot the scene in the morning, when the tide was out. Roger waited until the afternoon, when the tide was smashing up against large rocks. We were both trying to remain standing and play the scene while stumbling around. Somehow, I ran my little toe into a rock and broke it, and

From the cult sci-fi film It Came from Outer Space.
(AUTHOR'S COLLECTION)

We look like the original ghostbusters in this photo from the 1957 drive-in classic Attack of the Crab Monsters. (AUTHOR'S COLLECTION)

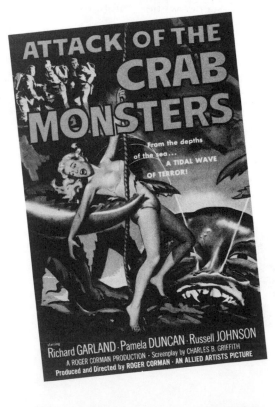

Corman had some guy on the set—not a first-aid technician, mind you—tape up my toe quickly with gaffer's tape and said, "All right, back in the water. Let's do it again."

With such piddly budgets and small crews, he was forced to improvise. And he didn't pay well, either.

It's absolutely amazing to me that the sci-fi films I made eons ago have become popular over the years. I thought they would die the minute they came out, but *Crab Monsters* ended up making a million dollars. I have to admit, Roger Corman did some amazing things with what little he had. Roger is an important man in film history. He gave many young actors, like Jack Nicholson, their break. He was a directorial tutor to such greats as Peter Bogdanovich, Joe Dante, Martin Scorsese, and Ron Howard.

I'll tell you what I really am proud of during those years. I did two terrific episodes of "The Twilight Zone," which, at that time, was a powerful show with a great audience. It was considered a "prestige" show, and working with Rod Serling was wonderful. He was kind of a quiet, charming, self-contained guy who came from upstate New York, near where I grew up. So we had something in common to talk about.

In one brain-twisting "Twilight Zone" episode titled "Back There," I played a man who retreated in time to the night Lincoln was assassinated at Ford's Theatre; I desperately tried to prevent the President from being shot. In the episode titled "Execution," Albert Salmi played a guy in the Old West who is about to be hanged, and with my time machine, I yanked him out of the year 1850 abruptly and plopped him into modern-day New York City. The guy ended up being so disoriented, he tried to shoot a jukebox.

I appeared as a guest star on quite a few of those vintage TV anthologies during the exciting time of live television, like "Playhouse 90," "Studio One," and "Climax." Those shows were wonderful. Later, I had roles on "Alfred Hitchcock Presents," "Death Valley Days," "Ben Casey," "Gunsmoke," and "Route 66," among many others. I only regret not being able to appear on any "Star Trek" episodes, although I was up for a role a few times. That was disappointing because I'm a trekkie.

In the 1957 Roger Corman film Rock All Night. (AUTHOR'S COLLECTION)

With Edward G. Robinson and Warren Stevens in the 1954 film Black Tuesday. (AUTHOR'S COLLECTION)

I also enjoyed the "Outer Limits" episode I appeared in and Boris Karloff's "Thriller," which costarred William Shatner. I acted in a sprinkling of film and television Westerns before I landed the role of Marshal Gib Scott on the TV series "Black Saddle" with Peter Breck. While under contract to Universal, I did a number of westerns with Audie Murphy, and one in particular that comes to mind starred Ronald Reagan: *Law and Order.*

I didn't have any choice in the matter, because I was under contract to Universal at the time, and what I objected to was Reagan's politics. He may be a sweet man otherwise, but there were political views that we violently disagreed on. When he became president of the Screen Actors Guild, I disagreed with many of his decisions. Politically, he's been an anathema to me.

We made *Law and Order* in 1952. It was released in 1953, during the McCarthy era, while the Red Scare was fully enflamed around

In 1962, Jack Webb narrated TV's "General Electric True," which presented weekly dramas based on actual documented accounts. In this episode, James Griffith is my patrol aide and I am a Union Army sharpshooter who attempts an unprecedented long-range rifle shot at a Confederate general. (AUTHOR'S COLLECTION)

I was U.S. Marshal Gib Scott on TV's "Black Saddle." (AUTHOR'S COLLECTION)

With my costar Anna Lisa in TV's "Black Saddle." (AUTHOR'S COLLECTION)

Hollywood. And I was one of those people being hounded. I was not a Communist, but because I had attended the Actors Lab, which was labeled a Communist-front organization, I was accused of being a Communist sympathizer, a "fellow traveler."

Back then, Reagan saw Red every time he turned around, and he made note of it when I worked with him in this Western. He was suspicious of everyone—unless you were a John Wayne–like, ultra 110 percent American conservative.

You have to realize that that was a dangerous time in this country. People's freedoms were being inhibited and challenged, and in those years you were guilty by association or accusation—unless you proved yourself innocent. Reagan was a part of that.

A scene with actress Ruth Hampton in the 1953 film Law and Order. (AUTHOR'S COLLECTION)

In the 1953 version of Law and Order *I shot Ronald Reagan in the shoulder. I love that film.* (AUTHOR'S COLLECTION)

In this film, Alex Nicol, Reagan, and I played brothers. Reagan was the sheriff, Nicol was more of a peacemaker, and I was the heavy. During the filming, Reagan constantly referred to people he thought were "pinko," and I can remember that Alex and I spoke up a few times. We told him he was going overboard. Reagan told us, "Oh no, you guys are naive. You don't know. There are people trying to take over the country, and they have to be stopped!"

This whole period in America made me sick. I remember that later I did a guest spot on "The Real McCoys" and Walter Brennan approached me one day and asked me to sign some kind of loyalty oath he was holding in his hand. I refused. I thought, "Why do I have to prove to anybody that I'm a patriot?" I had served my time overseas during World War II. I was shot down and earned a Purple Heart, risking my life. Hell, I understand Reagan never even left the country during the war. He was stationed at "Fort Roach," making military training films at the old Hal Roach Studios in Culver City, California.

GETTING MAROONED

I suffered incredible agonies for months . . .
nearly everything went wrong.
                    —SHERWOOD SCHWARTZ

S H E R W O O D Schwartz isn't exactly sure where the inspiration for "Gilligan's Island" came from. He read *Robinson Crusoe* when he was young, and he recalls a class in college that posed the question: "What one thing would you wish for if you were deserted on an island?" Maybe there's a little bit of William Golding's *Lord of the Flies* in there, too.

In the spring of 1963, Schwartz, a former writer for Red Skelton and Bob Hope, created seven characters and typed them up as a "bible" for a show he was about to launch. He plucked the name for the show's title right out of the Los Angeles white pages, figuring "Gilligan" would insure the correct attitude because "it's a happy name that was also funny," he says. And, most important, he wanted to portray cliché characters who could be easily identified as social surrogates.

Sound overly philosophical for "Gilligan's Island"? Maybe. It was surprising to me when I found out years later that the characters were prototypes of sectors of society. These characters marooned on an island together were not lukewarm personifications that left any questions in the mind of the viewer—except the ponderances about the luggage and other logical aspects that surfaced.

Sherwood explains: "Our cast of characters was not lukewarm. They were hot. They were easily identifiable. Our bumbling hero was the most bumbling you ever saw. Our rich man was a billionaire. And the professor knew absolutely everything."

Someone once said that the inhabitants on "Gilligan's Island" represented a variation of the seven deadly sins. Actually, they were broad caricatures of characters we've seen on countless disaster movies. Sherwood intentionally organized this diverse group of exaggerated crazies to mirror the American melting pot—all cooking under the pressure of being completely isolated from civilization. "A social microcosm," Sherwood called it when he sat in front of network executives, who had blank stares on their faces.

When Sherwood put his master's degree in psychology to work and explained his elaborate basis to the folks at CBS, no one realized the show he was pitching would become the most rerun show of all time—a show about a three-hour tour that would last three seasons and then be sentenced to a life of eternal syndication.

Keep in mind that the notion of syndication, or reruns, was so fresh at the time that many shows were just shelved after they left the air—never to be seen again until the 1990s, when a programming-starved medium called "cable" would play them out of desperation. And they make money.

I don't think the innocuous world of "Gilligan's Island" requires scholarly extrapolation. But it is astounding that "Gilligan's Island" has been the topic of many dissertations that attempt to reveal hidden meanings which eagerly address social issues and philosophical themes.

Sherwood Schwartz's agony started when he got the go-ahead to make a pilot, even though Jim Aubrey, the president of CBS, detested the idea from the start. There were other executives in the network who loved it, like Hunt Stromberg, Jr., and Mike Dann. Sherwood says that Aubrey unsuccessfully pestered him to change the whole show right up until the time it premiered. Other CBS brass started meddling as well, and by the time Sherwood's idea was finished getting beat up in many high-level meetings, it looked nothing like he had intended.

One guy wanted the show to involve the S.S. *Minnow* charter boat setting out on a new adventure cruise each week—with guest stars. (And this was years before "The Love Boat" set sail.) Another

Sherwood Schwartz (with glasses) proudly poses with his cast and director Jack Arnold on the set of "The Friendly Physician." (Notice Bob is concealing a cigarette from the camera.) (COURTESY OF SHERWOOD SCHWARTZ.)

executive pushed the intelligent idea of having Gilligan befriend a talking dinosaur on the other side of the island. "It would be another 'Mister Ed'!"

Sherwood nearly pulled his hair out at every meeting. His perseverance paid off, and he began making his pilot, just about the way he wanted to, in a remote section of Kauai, Hawaii, not far from some of the tropical-paradise background seen in the film *South Pacific*. At a cost of $175,000, the pilot was completed and shipped to New York for approval, with hopes for a purchase by the network.

They hated it. It was rejected and returned with no explanation.

Sherwood reclaimed the actual reel of film and redid the pilot. He recast the parts of the Professor, Ginger, and Mary Ann, reedited the pilot with a new theme song, and resubmitted it to CBS. The test audiences loved it. In fact, CBS tested the pilot over and over again to see if there were a problem with the audience; the network was bewildered by the overwhelming appeal.

At the eleventh hour, Jim Aubrey conceded and put this uncharted island on the network map for the fall 1964 season.

Casting was a headache, says Sherwood. Although he had a few people in mind for these roles—like Jim Backus and Natalie Schafer for Mr. and Mrs. Howell—he came up blank for Gilligan, Skipper, Ginger, and the rest.

Originally, Sherwood pursued Jerry Van Dyke for the part of Willy Gilligan. (That was Sherwood's intended first name for Gilligan if it were necessary to mention one. It never came up on any episode, however.) Jerry Van Dyke rejected the idea and was known for many years as the star of the "worst show on television," something called "My Mother the Car." Nearly twenty-five years later he became a big hit in "Coach," which completely revitalized his career.

The William Morris office suggested Bob Denver for Gilligan, and after meeting this television beatnik, Sherwood put his skepticism aside and thought, "This guy might work."

Casting the Skipper was agonizing, Sherwood says, because it was imperative that the relationship between Gilligan and Skipper have perfect chemistry, Sherwood explained: "I knew the Skipper would be yelling at Gilligan all the time and, as it turned out, hitting him on the head with his hat. I needed somebody who could sincerely play a Skipper, who would remain lovable and warm, no matter how much he yelled at his true friend Gilligan."

Sherwood wrote a test scene that had the Skipper ripping Gilligan apart. He figured if any actor survived that with some decency and integrity intact, then that would be Jonas Grumby, aka the Skipper. Even ol' Archie Bunker didn't look right. It's true. Carroll O'Connor was among the many heavy-set men who tested for the role.

Jim Backus took a gamble and agreed to play Thurston Howell III only if CBS doubled its offer. Sherwood and the network knew Jim was fantastic for the part, so CBS immediately approved the request and picked up the extra funds. Jim had worked with Sherwood on radio and TV before and took the role without even reading the script.

"I figured if it's good enough for Sherwood, it's good enough for me," Jim said. "So when we got on this little plane to Hawaii to film the pilot, I found out that my part was, well, the wine list was longer. Sherwood said, 'Don't worry, we'll fix it up.' So between us we sat there and figured out some pretty good rich gags and such."

It was getting close to the time to depart for Hawaii, and Sherwood still didn't have a Skipper. Then one night, Sherwood and his wife, Mildred, were out for dinner and saw Alan Hale, Jr., from across the restaurant.

"That's him." Sherwood knew it.

After he went through the proper channels of contacting talent for a job via an agent, Hale was summoned to test for the Skipper. Believe it or not, even though Alan was working in a film at the time, he was in a lull in his career and seriously considering trying a new profession. Alan explained how he barely made it to the test:

> I was up in Saint George, Utah, with Audie Murphy doing a movie. I had a call for Sunday to make this test, but I also had a problem getting off the set. How was I gonna get outta there? A pal of mine, we took a couple of horses and rode onto the main road, and he took the horses back. I hitchhiked from there to Las Vegas and took an airplane to Los Angeles and then a cab to the studio. I went through four states to get to that test.
>
> When I got there, Mr. Sherwood Schwartz said, "Alan, it was so nice of you to come in for this. I wrote this part for you, so you are definitely the Skipper if you so desire. I just want to see you with these other people." I was flattered. He put me up front like that.

THE TALE OF THE FIRST FATEFUL TRIP

Imagine this: You're an actor, and you land a role on a series. You make the pilot, and then the officials look at it and approve it only after they've singled you out and said, "But we don't want you." That's bloody devastating!

Only Sherwood Schwartz and maybe a few network executives know the real reason why three of the roles were recast. And I must be careful what I say here because I don't want to offend anyone. For many years, I've protected the actors who originally played Ginger, Mary Ann, and the Professor. In interviews, people would ask me who played the original Professor and I'd say, "I don't know." But I knew who he was, and I knew his work.

When Turner Broadcasting unearthed this half-hour pilot film from its vaults and premiered it on October 16, 1992, on TBS, the world finally found out who these rejected actors were.

John Gabriel played the high school teacher known as "the Professor," a blonde actress named Kit Smythe played Ginger, and Nancy McCarthy played Bunny, a secretary. There was no Mary Ann yet. The film was produced in a joint venture among United Artists, CBS, Sherwood, and Phil Silvers's company, Gladasya Productions. (Gladasya was a twist on Silvers's famous catchphrase, "Glad t' see ya!" that stemmed from the days of burlesque and became even more popular when he played Sergeant Bilko on "The Phil Silvers Show.")

If you get an opportunity to see the pilot, you may agree with me when I note the difference between the Professor in the pilot and my Professor. I think my Professor Roy Hinkley was more of a reassuring man. Also, Ginger and Bunny were not played anything like the characters Tina Louise and Dawn Wells enacted.

Friday, November 22, 1963, was the last day of filming on the beach at Moloa'a Bay. It was late in the morning when someone came running down to the company and said that they just heard on the radio that President Kennedy had been shot. Filming staggered on, Sherwood recalls. "No one could believe the news."

Between scenes, everyone crowded around the radio listening to news bulletins, and tears streamed from most of their eyes. The next thing they heard was that Lyndon Johnson was being sworn in as President, and they all knew there was no miscommunication.

An eerie proof of that day can be seen in any of the first season's black and white episodes. Don't blink, but if you watch the opening theme from any of those shows, in the harbor scene where the S.S. *Minnow* sets sail, there is a flag flying at half-mast in the background.

The S.S. Minnow *really was a tiny ship. Where did the Howells sleep during the storm? And what about that car in the background? (© 1993* CBS, INC.*)*

These rare photographs of the original cast were taken in Hawaii on the day that President Kennedy was assassinated. Above, from left to right: Jim Backus, Natalie Schafer, Nancy McCarthy, John Gabriel, Kit Smythe, Bob Denver, and Alan Hale, Jr. (PERSONALITY PHOTOS, INC.)

Lovey: *Oh, darling, I always knew you had a heart.*

Thurston: *Yes, remind me to speak to the Professor. There must be a painless way to turn it back to stone.*

(PHOTO BY GABI RONA)

* * *

Natalie Schafer says when she got back from Hawaii, she completely forgot about the pilot. "I guess it was Christmastime or New Year's that I went down to Puerto Vallarta with a group of friends, and my mother was very ill at the time," she said. "I was very nervous about going away at the time, and I thought something might happen to her. My friends convinced me the trip would be good for me.

"One day we were sitting having drinks at the hotel when a telegram was brought to me. I opened it and burst into tears! Everybody thought it was my mother, and they all came around me and said, 'Don't worry, we'll get you back.' And I cried and said, 'No, no, no—the series sold!' "

CBS put Sherwood's island on the air, and Dawn, Tina, and I joined the cast. Sherwood fought the network's strange decision to air "Two on a Raft," the *second* episode filmed, as the premiere show on September 26, 1964, as it made sense that the pilot, for which we shot new scenes at Zuma Beach, California, should air first to tell the story of the shipwreck.

Later on, Sherwood utilized some of the pilot's footage in the first season's Christmas show (the twelfth episode, "Birds Gotta Fly, Fish Gotta Talk"), in which the cast flashes back to their first day on the island. A very strange blooper is in that episode. Look very closely at the scene of Gilligan sleeping on the boat, waking up when he hears Skipper calling him. The other passengers asleep on the boat are clearly the original Professor, Ginger, and Bunny. No one caught that.

TESTING, TESTING

~~~~~~

RAQUEL WELCH AS MARY ANN?
DABNEY COLEMAN PLAYING THE PROFESSOR?

BELIEVE it or not, Raquel Welch and Dabney Coleman tested for roles in "Gilligan's Island," but for some reason they weren't chosen to take the three-hour tour on "TV's *Titanic*," as the show has been called many times. I was *this* close to missing the boat myself. I rejected the offer to make a test film for it twice before I gave in. Why? I guess it was ego. I was waiting for Godot, not Gilligan.

Just before "Gilligan's Island" got under way, the roles of the Professor, Mary Ann, and Ginger were being recast. My agent, Sid Gold, called me twice, advising me that Hal Cooper, a friend of mine, had suggested to Sherwood Schwartz that I might be suitable as the Professor in this bizarre show the network had purchased. Sid urged me to go in and make the test. But I didn't want to. I was at a point in my career where I was being considered for the lead in a television series. I had already costarred in "Black Saddle" for two years on the network. I was thirty-nine years old. It was deciding time. It was time to make a move.

What really held me back was that I had been seriously considered for the role of Dr. Ben Casey. Jim Moser, the creator of "Ben Casey," liked my audition, but I lost out to Vince Edwards. A little later on, I had made a pilot film with Jane Powell, the former child actress from MGM. It was about Powell, now a grown woman who was in show business, and I played a college professor. It didn't sell.

Really, I was waiting for something else. I was waiting for my shot, and the idea of being one of seven didn't appeal to me at all. Sid Gold agreed that my role of a lifetime had not yet come along. The offer still stood, but I again refused Sherwood Schwartz.

That went on for weeks, and Sid called again, telling me that Sherwood really wanted me to come in and at least test. "What have you got to lose?"

I gave in. It was not the caliber of work I was searching for, but I went in and tried out for the cameras.

Alan Hale was in the studio waiting for me with a script in his hand. There was a little five-minute scene Skipper and I did for the cameras against a blank background. At that time, the show's sets had not been built. The producers just wanted to see what I looked like on camera, my presence on film, my delivery. Meanwhile, there were streams of women testing opposite Bob Denver for the roles of Mary Ann and Ginger. Raquel Welch was one of the women who read for Mary Ann—not Ginger, as you might think. Eventually, Dawn Wells was handed the role of Mary Ann, and someone for Ginger had yet to be chosen.

When I went home after the test, I looked at my wife, at my two kids, and at my house up in the hills in Studio City. I wasn't making millions of dollars so that I could go forever without working. I had to work, so I figured I'd better accept this damned thing. I had to sign a preliminary contract with the studio even before the test. This was standard because the producers didn't want any actors holding them up once they got the role.

The stage manager working on my test was a friend of mine, Sam Gary, whom I had known from way back. He did me the favor of arranging the order of the tests because I wasn't the only guy the network executives were looking at. Sam assembled the films with particular strategy: First, he put a pretty good test, then a lousy test,

These were the first official cast portraits, taken in the exclusive picturesque area of Franklin Canyon, near Beverly Hills. (PHOTOS BY GABI RONA)

then me, and finally a mediocre test. He positioned me just right, and the powers that be chose me.

Ethel Winant, CBS's head of casting, called me to say the role was mine. Ethel was a petite woman, strong and intelligent, who later went on to PBS and did wonderful things there. It was highly unusual at that time to have a woman in such a powerful position in the network. (There wasn't even a woman's restroom in the offices when she started at CBS. She had to use the men's room and leave her high heels outside the door so everyone would know she was in the bathroom.) But it was easy to see why Ethel was there. She was one tough cookie, and she knew what she was doing. And fortunately, my wife, Kay, and I had known Ethel for years.

When Ethel called to inform me of a very strange request, she simply laid it on the line: "Look, Russell, I've got to talk to you. Hunt Stromberg wants to see you in his office, and he wants you stripped down to your shorts."

"What the hell does that mean?" I asked her.

"Hunt wants to see what you look like, so he can make a final decision."

She was speaking of Hunt Stromberg, Jr., the West Coast vice president for program development at CBS. He was an integral force in getting "Gilligan's Island" on the air, so Sherwood asked me to appease him any way I possibly could. I only go so far, however. I had heard about other actors who had filmed tests for him in their underwear, but I was not going to join that lineup. I told Ethel to forget it. I could be very frank with her.

"Look, I'm a serious actor," I said in our phone conversation. "You know me. I'm not interested in that. I'm fit. I've got a good body."

Ethel said, "I know you do. But why not just go meet with him?"

I told her if that personal peek is what it took to get the part, I'd decline. Later in the day, Ethel called me again and said, "I'll tell you what. If you come to my office and take your shirt off, I'll tell Hunt I saw you and that will be that." So I agreed. When I got to CBS, Ethel stood there looking at me with my shirt clenched in my hand and a smile on my face. We laughed about it. "I know this is

(PHOTO BY GABI RONA)

ridiculous, but I'm going to take a Polaroid and just give this to him. Will that be all right?"

I smiled for the camera, and that was the end of it.

I think the main concern was whether or not CBS wanted the Professor to *have* some sex appeal or *not* to have any sexual allure at all. It was a matter of smooth chest or hairy chest, I think.

Ethel Winant remembers that the last character to be cast was Ginger. "The whole process became so involved, it grew legs and became a monster," Ethel says. Her casting search extended from one coast to the other. "We tested every girl we could find for Ginger, but nobody quite looked right until we found Tina Louise, who was in a Broadway play at the time."

It was Ethel who orchestrated the contract release for Tina so she could move from New York to Los Angeles and start in on the series.

Finally, on June 9, 1964, Tina signed a contract with CBS and Sherwood had his seven stranded Castaways.

Problems arose almost immediately. "They told me the series was about a movie star who got stranded on an island with a few others," Tina says. She hesitantly agreed to perform the role because she was bound by her contract. According to Tina, there was a breakdown in communication when she was cast as Ginger. She says she was told that she would be the star of "Gilligan's Island," and the rest of us would be the supporting cast.

"Ginger was proposed as an Eve Arden type, but I didn't think it would work—or work for me personally," Tina says. "I didn't think they would accept a bitchy character as such. I always enjoyed my scenes once they started writing them for the Marilyn Monroe type. Then it was fine."

Tina says that originally Ginger was also described to her as a Marilyn Monroe–Lucille Ball type. Sherwood Schwartz shakes his head at that one. "Marilyn Monroe, maybe," he says, "but the only resemblance to Lucy would be the color of their hair."

We gathered for the first reading of our first show at the CBS studios in a conference room around a huge table with Sherwood Schwartz at the helm. I looked around and this is what I saw: across the table was my friend Alan Hale, whom I had worked with in his series "Casey Jones" several years earlier. He ended up being the "rock" of our show. And there was Bob Denver, a fine comic actor who had made me laugh when I watched "The Many Loves of Dobie Gillis" on television.

Sitting next to me was a beautiful girl with big brown eyes named Dawn Wells, so sweet and charming and sexy. And Tina Louise, the other beauty on the show, tall, with flowing red hair and confidence.

Dear Natalie Schafer sat next to her costar, Jim Backus. They acted as if they had known each other for years, but it had only been a few months. Natalie was a funny lady, down-to-earth, elegant, and intelligent. And, of course, the great Jim Backus—"Mr. Magoo"— with his long list of film credits. I knew him mostly as a serious film actor, so watching him joke and laugh and carry on gregariously was a surprise. Jim was "a fellow of infinite jest."

Next to Sherwood was our director, John Rich, one of the best in the business. He had just completed directing two seasons of the popular "Dick Van Dyke Show" and was going to be our coproducer as well as our director. Our "creator," Sherwood Schwartz, whom I came to know as a first-class gentleman, was a man who cared about his work and about his actors. It was clear that this man was hard-working and willing to listen to our ideas.

Maybe we all had something after all.

(PHOTO BY GABI RONA)

THE CASTAWAYS

ALAN HALE was just as he appeared on the show: a bear-huggy kind of guy. He was a big man with a tight frame and a gliding, broad stride in his walk. He was agile, lovable, and sincere, and these qualities were topped with a bubbly, outgoing jolliness that you rarely see in people—except maybe Santa Claus. These qualities made him very approachable. Really. That was his public persona, and it's why it was such a pleasure to work with him every day.

Alan and I were very good friends on the set, but I don't know what he was like at home. I'm sure he had as full a range of emotions as any human being. His wife, Trinket, says he had a private "fragileness" about him that not many people saw. "Alan liked his solitude," she said. "If he ever got mad or irritated, he liked to be alone. He was sensitive. Things people said could easily hurt him, although he didn't let on. You know, people can be unfeeling sometimes." Alan was a father, a husband, an actor. And God knows what goes on in one's personal life. As an actor, you try not to bring that to work with you. You leave your problems at home. Alan was proficient at that. Not that he had many problems, but if he did, no one ever detected it.

In the course of "Gilligan's Island," I had Alan and Trinket over

There was a serious side to Alan that was seldom seen by the public.
(COURTESY OF SHERWOOD SCHWARTZ)

for dinner a few times, and my experiences with him were always memorable. On the set he was 100 percent pro and of good spirit. Always. And over the years, it was amazing, but one thing stuck out: This guy never seemed to age.

Very simply, Alan made me feel good when I was around him. He had an infectious, deep, hearty laugh that you would recognize across a large room. It was on a sound level all its own, booming over everybody else's laughter.

Alan was an encompassing kind of person, and he had a lot of friends because he grew up in Hollywood in a family that was rooted

It was rare to see Alan in anything but a playful mood. (AUTHOR'S COLLECTION)

in the entertainment business. He loved to host parties and have friends and fans stop in to see him at his West Hollywood restaurant, Alan Hale's Lobster Barrel, with which he was associated for about fifteen years after "Gilligan's Island" ended.

I think that everybody who ever worked with Alan loved him. He seemed to know everybody in town. John Wayne. Bette Davis. Jimmy Stewart. James Cagney. John Ford. Even Walter Cronkite. *Everybody*. They were all good friends of his. He was very affectionate, whether it was with friends, colleagues, or fans. And I suspect his father, Alan Hale, Sr., was that way, too. Many people used to confuse Alan with his father. I'm not sure why, but sometimes Alan dropped the "Jr." in his credits. Even when he signed autographs, he'd tag on the "Jr." occasionally, but not always.

His father was a successful actor in films dating back to the silent days of Valentino and D. W. Griffith. The senior Hale had worked with Errol Flynn in a few motion pictures, and he played Little John in *The Adventures of Robin Hood*. And he was the fellow driving the car that picks up Clark Gable and Claudette Colbert in the Frank Capra *It Happened One Night.*

I think Alan regretted not being able to work with his father in the craft they shared. They were supposed to do an RKO movie together called *At Sword's Point,* but, suddenly, Alan's father died just before the production began in 1950. Alan's respect and love for his father was evident, even when fans mistook him for his father. And if fans were wise to the difference, they might ask Alan permission to inquire about his late father. Alan was so polite about it. He'd smile and say, "Yes indeed, feel free. How kind of you," and really anticipate their inquisitiveness.

Alan Hale, Sr., and his son, Alan Hale, Jr., in 1948. At some point in their lives they looked almost exactly alike. (COURTESY OF MRS. ALAN HALE, JR.)

In reality, Alan loved the sea. He respected it. His wife said he "had a karma with it." (COURTESY OF MRS. ALAN HALE, JR.)

If you look closely, you'll notice a reminder of his father in every episode of "Gilligan's Island." Alan faithfully wore an emerald and diamond pinky ring that had belonged to his father.

There is no question that Alan Hale, Jr., will be best remembered as the Skipper. He immortalized that very nautical rank. What other Skipper *is* there? It was such a fitting role for him because Alan Hale, Jr., was of the sea. He believed he had a karma with it. After all, he was a Pisces who loved and respected the sea. And when the time came, he said he wanted to be cremated and have his ashes scattered at sea.

Alan was nearly sixty-eight years old when he died on January 2, 1990, leaving his wife, four children, grandchildren, a long list of film and television credits, and more fans than can be counted.

The last time I saw Alan was on one of our personal appearances together in New York. After the appearance, Bob, Dawn, Alan, and I were all taken to the airport in a limousine, and when we arrived at the main terminal of JFK, we all said our good-byes right there because our flights were jetting off in different directions.

I didn't know what was wrong with him at the time, but it was evident he was ill because of his drastic weight loss. I kept asking Bob, "What's wrong with Alan?" and Bob said, "I don't know. He won't discuss it."

My last glimpse of Alan was watching him walk through the terminal toward his gate. As usual, he was wearing his cap and carrying a small bag over his shoulder. I stood there and watched him for a while. Alan walked very slowly, and he slumped over a bit. I knew that he was a sick man. It saddened me.

Trinket said Alan was sick almost two years before anybody knew it. He carried his illness with dignity. He even hid it from her, until she found a string of doctor's bills for treatment of cancer of the thymus.

Trinket remembers Alan's last day:

In the hospital, Alan said to me, "Honey, you remember what I want, don't you?" And I assured him I did. When Alan died, I was in the room with his sister and the hospital priest. Right outside his room you could see a church steeple in the

(PHOTO BY GABI RONA)

distance. I looked out the window at the steeple and prayed that if he couldn't get well that God would take him. I hoped He would take him at sunset. Alan would have wanted that. By that time, Alan was unconscious and peaceful.

Honest, just as the sun went down, Alan opened his eyes and looked at me. I leaned in to him and said, "I love you," and then he took a deep breath and he died. The priest said, "I think we've all just witnessed a miracle."

Dawn called me in the morning when she found out that Alan had died. Dawn was like another daughter to him, and I know it was crushing for her. She had been to the hospital to see him the day before, and she said she knew it wouldn't be long. All of us felt the loss of a dear friend.

Later on, I found out that although the Coast Guard had called Trinket and offered a full military service at sea, she declined and thanked them for their kindness. Trinket fulfilled Alan's wishes, through the Neptune Society; he was cremated and his ashes were scattered at sea. Wouldn't you know it, a helicopter for one of the tabloids hovered above, photographing the whole thing.

Trinket arranged an intimate ceremony on a charter boat, with family and kids gathered, and Dawn represented all of us from the show. After some passages from the Bible were read, his ashes were distributed and flowers were scattered on the water. The Skipper was at sea.

I miss Alan.

BOB DENVER couldn't be more different from Gilligan, which attests to the fact that he's one fine actor.

He is not bumbling, or inept, or stupid like Gilligan. Rather, Bobby, as we sometimes called him, is a highly intelligent, well-read gentleman, who takes his work very seriously. He was not at all flip about the silly things he had to do as Gilligan. All of his actions, every nuance, every giggle, every gesture and movement, were well calculated and executed with unshakable confidence. Now, I ask you—does that sound like Gilligan?

Bob has an inborn sense of comedic timing that you can't *give* to anybody, and "Gilligan's Island" proved to audiences what an accomplished, gifted actor he is.

Bob and I are good friends, but I would not say we're bosom buddies. Our families didn't socialize or share Thanksgiving dinners. Our kids didn't play together after school. We have always been more businesslike, but on a warm, friendly basis. I have always admired Bob for his talent, and I think that his wife, Dreama, whom he married after the show ended, really changed his life for the better. And Bob is a family man, with beautiful daughters who just love their father. Bob and Dreama have a young, disabled son, and it's refreshing to see the dedication they have to his well-being and happiness.

Bob was a grade school teacher before he decided to make a go of it as an actor. He has a degree in political science from Loyola University and for a time studied law there as well. While he was at Loyola, he discovered the Del Ray Players and began working with this theater group in a comedy relief part in *The Caine Mutiny*. When he graduated he soon found that jobs were not easy to obtain, so he taught history and arithmetic at Corpus Christi Children's School in Pacific Palisades, California. On the side, he coached football, basketball (boys and girls), and baseball. Then he suddenly came into a very good thing.

He was cast as the lazy beatnik, Maynard G. Krebs, which, for a while, was his most famous role. It's still popular with fans of "The Many Loves of Dobie Gillis," which continues to rerun today. Directly after that series ended, Bob slid into the lagoon.

Although Bob later did Broadway (replacing Woody Allen in *Play it Again, Sam*) and a string of motion pictures, he's now resigned to the fact that he'll always be known as either Maynard or Gilligan. In the past fifteen years he has reprised both characters for TV reunion movies—with ambivalence, I know.

When we reunited for the "Rescue from Gilligan's Island" TV movie, Bob was forty-three, and he once again slipped into his long-sleeved red rugby shirt and bleached-out bell-bottoms. He colored his graying hair and put on the rumpled white cap for another adventure as one of the original boat people. He did a fantastic job,

*Sometime after they had left the island, Alan guest-starred on Bob's series,
"The Good Guys."* (PERSONALITY PHOTOS, INC.)

and philosophized: "You really can't go back and capture what you
did—not really. I don't care when you try."

Many times since then Bob has been seen in both motion pictures
and television as Gilligan. I think in the back of his mind, he wishes
he weren't so indelibly associated with Gilligan. At the same time, I
think he's grateful for the recognition. He knows "Gilligan's Island"
is an inseparable part of Americana now.

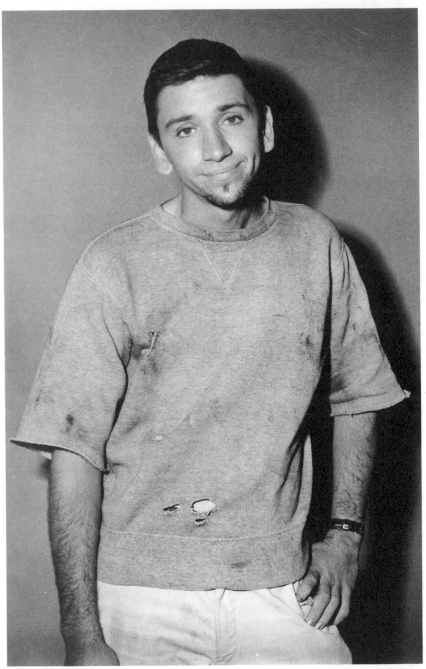

Before Gilligan came along, Bob became famous as Maynard G. Krebs, the beatnik who hated the word "work," in "The Many Loves of Dobie Gillis."
(PHOTO BY GABI RONA)

*Kids at heart: Dawn and
Bob in a dream sequence.*
(PERSONALITY PHOTOS, INC.)

*Bob's son, Patrick, made
his acting debut in one of
our episodes.* (PERSONALITY
PHOTOS, INC.)

Bob says: "I meet fathers who grew up with it and watch with
their kids now. I always say to the dads or the moms, 'I know what
you say to them when you watch it.' And they look at me and say,
'What?' I tell them, 'You always say, "Okay, here comes the good
part!"' Each show had one real good part—one big special effect
or gag."

BOB DENVER ON THE BROAD COMEDY

When we began "Gilligan's Island," I really wanted to do physical comedy and all the bad gags that go along with it because I knew I could do it. I really didn't do much of that in "Dobie Gillis." When we first tested for the Skipper and Alan Hale walked in, he was a good forty feet away, but we knew that he was the Skipper and we knew this kind of stuff was going to click with him. He was so strong, I could run across the stage and jump up and he would catch me like a feather without missing a beat. That's what made our comedy together so great.

I did a lot of broad stuff on "Gilligan," which, you know, you couldn't do except on a fantasy show like that. We could get away with anything—like the cartoon joke where the two natives were holding me up sitting on a board or something. They dropped the board, but I turned to the camera, looked for a second, then fell out of frame. Each week it was different, and that's what made it so much fun to do. Even the three years that we did the series, all I was doing was having a really great time doing that kind of comedy. Especially in the third year, when we started getting into more dream sequences and we got into costumes and we did some crazy stuff. The fourth year probably would have been even wilder.

JIM BACKUS told a spicy story one day on the "Gilligan's Island" set, and I have never forgotten it. He was near Beverly Hills, returning from an appointment one day, so he stopped in at the home of his good friend George Burns. Burns was sitting in his den, draped in a kimono, enjoying a cigar and martini while waiting for his butler to bring him a bowl of soup. George invited Jim to join him and relax for a while.

"Can I get you a cigar?" Burns asked.

(PHOTO BY GABI RONA)

"No, no, I just wanted to stop in and say hello," Jim replied.

"Let me have some soup brought in for you. It's great."

Jim shook his head. "No thanks, George. Henny and I are gonna go out for dinner."

"Let me make you a martini, then."

"No, really. I'll have one later."

"Then how 'bout a cup of coffee?"

"Thanks anyway, George."

George sipped his soup and both men sat there quietly. After a long pause, George finally looked up from his bowl.

"A little sex?"

Jim's sense of humor could be pretty raunchy sometimes. But not as dirty as he intended for the voice of his famous cartoon character, the myopic curmudgeon Mr. Magoo. He used to say, "The best of Magoo has to be censored."

Jim was notorious for ad-libbing while we filmed. Not all of it was lewd, but most of it was just plain hilarious. He'd tack on a line, or mumble a wisecrack, or he'd let out a Magoo-like bark that would have everybody in hysterics. He'd come up with a quick line or just a weird sound out of the blue that would just kill you. Some of that stuff had to be edited out. The scraps were combined with the rest of our filmed blunders for an outtake reel that was shown at the wrap party. Boy, would I like to have one of those reels now.

There were times on the set when Jim could be irascible and his feathers would get ruffled. Most of us could tell when to let him wander off into the hut and be alone to cool off. He rarely stayed in that mood. Most of the time Natalie could approach him about anything, and she would. They were very good friends, just like their characters.

One way to describe Jim's humor and his demeanor off camera is to compare his outrageousness with that of Jonathan Winters or Robin Williams, just less hyper.

It was wonderful to hear Jim reminisce about working in films and television with people like James Dean and Humphrey Bogart. I respected his résumé. His background in show business stretched back to the radio days, where his Thurston Howell originated. How-

Jim and Henny Backus were always madly in love with each other.
(COURTESY OF HENNY BACKUS)

ell was a refinement of his similarly snobbish radio character Hubert Updike III on "The Alan Young Show." Basically the same voice. Many of the same gags. And both sickeningly rich.

Before Sherwood Schwartz lured him into re-creating that character, Jim had appeared in quite a few guest spots on television. He starred opposite Joan Davis as the sedate Judge Bradley Stevens in "I Married Joan," which lasted three years. Mr. Magoo has had his own string of cartoons that have been well received since the 1950s. And in motion pictures, Jim made his mark in a few classics like *Rebel Without a Cause* and *It's a Mad, Mad, Mad, Mad World*, in which he played the drunken airplane pilot Tyler Fitzgerald, his favorite film role. In all, he did over fifty films. Kids today are stunned to see him in something dramatic or anything that deviates from Howell, but Jim was pretty adept at impressions. On "Gilligan's" I remember he managed a pretty good W. C. Fields once, and he wasn't bad at Ed Sullivan, either.

After we filmed "Rescue," Jim got pretty sick. All of a sudden, it seemed as if he had become a frail old man. He needed assistance to walk and move, and it seemed as if he was drained of energy. Jim

*Jim Backus based Thurston Howell III on a radio character he created in
the 1940s named Hubert Updike III.* (COURTESY OF HENNY BACKUS)

was very thin, and to a layman, his illness seemed like a stroke. His
mind was there, but, physically, he had a lot of problems. Evidently,
he had been suffering from a complication of afflictions that included agoraphobia (an abnormal fear of going out in public) and
Parkinson's disease. The whole thing wiped him out. As he described in *Backus Strikes Back*, a charming book he wrote in 1984
with his wife, Henny, he was unable to coordinate his arms and legs,
tie a tie, or even hold a fork.

He did strike back, to some extent, but the old Jim Backus never reappeared. When he was approached about recording some new Magoos for Saturday morning TV, he nearly declined out of fear and anxiety. Henny urged him to take the work, and, with hesitation, ol' Magoo had "done it again."

What brought him through his emotional and physical illnesses over the years was Henny's devotion. She kept him active, kept him going, and struggled to keep his spirits up, even though Jim's health was like a roller coaster for nearly ten years. Around Hollywood, they were known as quite a team, and theirs was a great love story.

If there is a snippet of film to prove Jim Backus was a first-rate dramatic actor, it might be this climactic scene from Rebel Without a Cause. *Jim played the pathetic father to James Dean's character. Ann Doran was Dean's mother.* (COURTESY OF HENNY BACKUS)

At the luau in the final scene of The Castaways on Gilligan's Island. (AUTHOR'S COLLECTION)

A frail Jim Backus in 1988. (PHOTO BY STEVE COX)

Jim Backus was the first of our cast to pass away. He died on July 3, 1989. To me, he had been ill for so long I never really thought it was going to happen. I preferred to remember the healthy, happy Jim whom I had known and enjoyed spending time with.

One of his obituaries reported, "If Backus had his way, Mr. Magoo would have died before him, not at the same time." Although I never heard Jim say it, I imagine he had a little resentment due to the nearsighted—and very popular—Quincy Magoo, who caused him to be typecast. Thurston Howell probably increased the aggravation a bit.

Don't let anyone kid you, though. He had a fond spot in his heart for Magoo. And Howell, too, by George.

NATALIE SCHAFER was a mystery to me at first. Here was this society lady, who, at first glance, seemed kind of phony. She seemed like a typical snooty Broadway diva, complete with a lorgnette—you know, those opera glasses with a long handle. She really used them for nearsightedness! Very quickly, I began to realize I had a mistaken impression. Once I got to know her, what emerged was a charming, funny, elegant lady who cared deeply about others.

Natalie was a woman who was very beautiful in her time. She had had a career in the theater long before she arrived in Hollywood and began making films at MGM, so her initial apprehension about "Gilligan's Island"—"that silly thing on TV"—was understandable.

Natalie was married just once, to actor Louis Calhern, in the thirties, and even after their divorce in the forties they remained good friends. I had met her husband in the fifties, so Natalie and I had some common ground for conversation. There's a funny story, actually, about Calhern's last wish. Literally on his deathbed, he pleaded with Natalie to finally reveal her age to him.

She looked him in the eye and said, "Never!"

That was a thing with Natalie. None of us knew how old she was when we worked together, nor did it really matter. When she died, we were all astounded at her age. Personally, I had no idea she was as old as she was. When I found out, it floored me. She never looked her age, and certainly she didn't act it.

(PHOTO BY GABI RONA)

Natalie was as dignified as she seemed on the show. (COURTESY OF NELL McCORMICK; NATALIE SCHAFER ESTATE)

Natalie told a reporter once, "They're talking too much about age nowadays. It seems to be so all-important when they ask, 'Is she forty?' 'Is she thirty?' 'Is she twenty?'—not 'Is she *good*?' And you watch some of the young people working today and they're chosen for age, not for ability. It's very shocking."

I remember Natalie telling me about the time she visited the doctor for a mandatory physical. She had to have a checkup for the studio's insurance, so she went back to the same doctor who had examined her years before.

He asked her, "Natalie, how old are you now?"

She said, "How old was I last time?"

There was even a close-ups clause in Natalie's contract for "Gilligan's Island" that prohibited any extreme close-ups of her face to be shot or shown on television. After a while I think she just forgot about that little notation in her contract, or she just decided she didn't care. There are a few close-ups.

There are a lot of famous Hollywood stories about Natalie. Some are rooted in truth, others in fiction—whichever she decided at the time she was retelling them. One tale she did tell on herself was of her great romance with the famous playwright George S. Kaufman—while he was still married. It seems she was Kaufman's mistress.

Evidently, after Natalie made her first film at MGM, *Reunion in France* (1942), Louis B. Mayer called her in to persuade her to sign a contract. He told Natalie, "We need somebody with dignity like you. A lady of elegance. We'll make you a star in motion pictures."

Natalie told Mayer she would love to, but she lived in New York and she was in love. Mayer said it would be no problem to bring her beau out to California as well, and she said, "Well, I don't think his wife would like that."

Mayer was shocked. He read her the riot act and said, "My God, I thought you were a lady! You're having an affair with a married man? Get out!" And she never signed on Mayer's dotted line.

Later on, when Natalie became Lovey Howell, it was evident why Sherwood had personally selected her. She was very much like Mrs. Howell; she dressed with great taste, and she enjoyed the best of both worlds—or coasts, you might say. During all the years I knew her, Natalie maintained a very nice Park Avenue apartment in Manhattan and she owned a house on Rodeo Drive in posh Beverly Hills. In both homes she stocked a small bar, and she loved to host parties. A number of years ago, when most of us in the cast were in New York for a reunion on "Good Morning America," Natalie invited us all over to her apartment for cocktails and we had a wonderful time being entertained by Mrs. Howell in grand style.

Natalie's most noticeable attribute was her trademark "rich" accent. That authentic accent, particularly some words, did not come easily when we were filming. Natalie showed up to work prepared, but she toiled over her "Gilligan's" scripts and struggled to learn her lines each week—more so than any of us, I think. She was just that kind of actor for whom memorization is definitely not instantaneous.

Natalie lived mostly at her home in Beverly Hills when she wasn't working and enjoyed spending time with friends who regularly popped over to chat, have a drink, and gossip. Nat hated being alone,

Natalie wasn't afraid to do or wear anything. (PHOTO BY SHERWOOD SCHWARTZ)

Natalie was like Mrs. Howell in whatever show she appeared. Here she plays a socialite on "Mayberry R.F.D." with George Lindsey as Goober. (COURTESY OF NATALIE SCHAFER ESTATE)

but as long as she had her tiny dogs, she was content. Sherwood remembered, "She was never without a little dog. She had one that lived to be fifteen, I think, and it was named Lovey. The last four or five years of Natalie's life, she had a cute little French poodle named Fifi, who was too small to jump up onto Natalie's bed. So Natalie had a ramp specially made so Fifi could walk up this ramp and get into bed with her at night."

Nothing fazed Natalie. She didn't hesitate to tell many people—including reporters—that although she had had a mastectomy many years ago, she never failed to swim nude in her pool every morning, wearing just a cap for her hair and gloves so the sun wouldn't cause age spots on her hands. She had no fear of intrusion because of the high wooden fences that surrounded the back of her California property. As I said, she was intractable, but in a divinely pleasant manner.

This was Natalie's bottle of Gilligan's Island vodka that she always kept refilled at her bar. (PHOTO BY STEVE COX)

Because of a recurring back ailment in her last few years, Natalie found solace from her extreme pain by fixing a Bloody Mary in the mornings and, when she felt the need, something more potent. There was an inconspicuous book wedged in among the rest in her small library. It was simply titled: *Joy.* And Natalie loved to have "Joy in the morning," but a few of us weren't sure what she meant. We found out later that there was a little flask secretly hidden inside the hollowed-out hardback.

I loved Natalie's sense of humor off screen. She was a determined, feisty woman who did exactly what she wanted. Just when you felt comfortable, she'd blurt out a shocking four-letter word just to catch you off guard, yet she retained her femininity. In conversation, she used to boast with a smile, ". . . because you know, I'm a bit of a bitch."

On April 10, 1990, Natalie died in her sleep. She was ninety years young.

TINA LOUISE was puzzling. She made it known when we were filming the series—and says it more often today—that she didn't like playing fiery Ginger Grant, but, on the other hand, she was stunningly perfect in the role. At one point, she even went to Jim Aubrey, then the president of CBS, and quit. But Aubrey—who was known as "The Smiling Cobra"—calmed her down. You would never have guessed there was discontent behind her fine work.

On any given day, we didn't know whether Tina was going to be Ginger Grant or Eva Grubb. When our show began drawing good audiences, we were all approached about making cast appearances on the "State and County Fair Circuit." The money would have been phenomenal for all of us. In just two weekends of appearances, we could have made thousands. The offer was for all seven of us or no offer at all. But for some reason, Tina was definitely not interested.

I must say, Tina's a damn good actress and we were lucky to have her in our ensemble because the role of Ginger was so difficult to cast. It had to be played just right. Not many people know that Tina studied acting with Lee Strasberg at the Actors Studio in New York at the same time as Joanne Woodward and a group of other talented students.

After "Gilligan's Island" was afloat on the network, Tina commented to *TV Guide*: "I'd heard about what series are like, but I really didn't know how it would be. I found that I couldn't use my work at all in this show. It was quite a shock. In this medium, you perform, everyone performs. There's no such thing as a real moment, an honest reaction, because the show is like a cartoon. You're not acting, not the way I studied it."

I don't agree with Tina on this. I think she did some fantastic acting on the show. That's not Tina on the screen—that's Ginger Grant, the femme fatale of the island. It's been said that Ginger Grant was the TV version of Marilyn Monroe. In fact, Tina might have been inspired by Marilyn when she played Ginger. "I was a great fan of Marilyn Monroe. I never met her," Tina said, "but I knew the quality she had and how to play it so it would work." Ginger was the first "vamp" introduced to boys and girls on television. Although there may be similarities between Tina the actress and Ginger the island movie queen, the two are definitely distinct.

Born Tina Blacker in New York City on February 11, 1938, she wasn't given a middle name. It wasn't until her acting teacher in high school gave her the name Louise, and Tina liked it so much, that she eventually adopted Louise as a professional name.

In interviews, Tina has described her childhood as very rigid and sometimes unhappy. Currently, she's thinking about putting her memories into a book that she'd like to call *Sundays*.

Her parents were divorced when she was very young, and at the age of five she was placed in a private boarding school that had visiting rights only on Sundays. She recently described the institution to writer Ronald Smith: "They didn't beat me. Just slapped me once. It was just a miserable place. And I don't think any child could really be happy between five and eight away from their parents, do you? No, I don't think so . . . they took away my dolls at night. It was a very confining atmosphere, not a particularly happy time."

Embracing the art of acting, Tina studied diligently in New York after she graduated from high school. Her talents landed her some choice roles on Broadway and off Broadway. She appeared in *The Fifth Season* in 1953 and *Li'l Abner* in 1956. In 1964 she was costarring with Carol Burnett in Broadway's *Fade Out—Fade In*

(PHOTO BY GABI RONA)

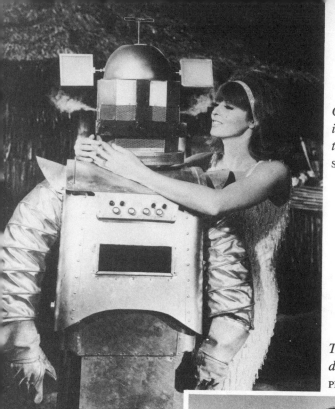

Ginger tries to arouse passion in a robot that has landed on the island. (COURTESY OF SHERWOOD SCHWARTZ)

Tina is a royal princess in a dream sequence. (PERSONALITY PHOTOS, INC.)

when she exited the show to move to California and become one of seven shipwrecked on a sitcom.

During the series, all of us in the cast attended Tina's wedding to talk-show host Les Crane, Jr., a pioneer in the audience-participation format that Phil Donahue has made popular. You know, the same blab-it-all style that runs amok on television these days. I remember Crane's talk show because it was strangely funny. He had a micro-

Tina Louise was a top model in New York in the early 1960s.
(JOEL RASMUSSEN COLLECTION)

phone mounted on a gunstock, like a shotgun, and he'd point it at people's faces, trying to elicit their reaction to some topic of the day. I couldn't believe it!

Tina and Crane were divorced while she was pregnant, and it took a lot of courage to raise a child as a single parent who was also trying to succeed in show business. Today it's evident that Tina is proud of the close-knit relationship she has with her lovely daughter, Caprice, now in her twenties. And it was Caprice who rekindled in her mom a little fascination for the old island after so many years.

Career-wise, Tina says she's most proud of her work in *God's*

Little Acre; *Friendships, Secrets and Lies*; and *The Stepford Wives*. She's also very proud of her dramatic performance in an episode of "Kojak" in which she played a drug addict. There have been a variety of roles that have come her way, but lingering in people's imagination is Ginger Grant.

People may assume Tina is violently opposed to Ginger, but now I think it's merely mild combat. Some of the reason for this partial reversal may be that Tina really hasn't changed much in her appearance over the years, which I'm sure pleases her. Fans recognize her daily. She still looks beautiful, and she has worked hard to maintain her figure. She still has the beauty mole on her left cheek and the flowing titian hair. ("Red is not a color I like," Tina says.)

DAWN WELLS has been called "pure Americana." Think of it: Her great-grandfather drove a stagecoach from Reno to Virginia City during the Gold Rush; she was Miss Nevada competing for the 1960 Miss America title; and we know her best as Mary Ann Summers, the homespun sweetheart from Horners Corners, Kansas, who lovingly baked coconut cream pies for six others stranded with her on an uncharted desert isle.

Dawn was the cast member who received the most fan mail while we were making "Gilligan's Island." There was something of an innocent, fresh, approachable, wholesome allure to Mary Ann that captured the hearts of many male fans during their youth. Well, I shouldn't limit that. Many fathers out there noticed Dawn's big brown eyes and long thick lashes, too. In many ways, pigtailed Mary Ann, in the gingham dress, was patterned after Dorothy in *The Wizard of Oz*. You can't get much more American than that.

This whole fascination was a surprise to Dawn, who assumed that the most beautiful character on the show was Ginger. As one writer put it, "Ginger Grant could make men swoon—a perfumed beauty in slinky gowns. But Mary Ann was a breath of fresh air in sporty short shorts . . . the girl next door."

You may be glad to know that Dawn Wells has always been very much like Mary Ann: kind, gentle, and extremely good with children. I think it's a shame Dawn didn't have any kids of her own, and I know she regrets it herself. She has said so. She was married for a

(PHOTO BY GABI RONA)

few years while we were doing the series, but that ended shortly after our show did and Dawn has remained single ever since.

I guess if I had to identify the one I was closest to in the cast, it would be Dawn. We've always shared a mutual fondness for one another. It was always platonic. At the outset, we were both ne- glected in the opening credits and referred to as "the rest," and our

Dawn demonstrated health and beauty tips for fan magazines during the 1960s. (PERSONALITY PHOTOS, INC.)

Not many know this, but Dawn Wells was a contestant in the Miss America Pageant in 1960. (PERSONALITY PHOTOS, INC.)

Is she angelic or what? (PHOTO BY GABI RONA)

roles were about the same proportion in the beginning. As time went by, I think the producers and writers began to realize that the Professor and Mary Ann were the lone voices of logic. We were very important to the show, and they expanded our parts.

Offstage, Dawn and I used to run lines together, and for me, that was a godsend because of those technical explanations. Dawn has said that the show was her training ground, but she could have fooled me. She didn't appear naive or inexperienced at all. In fact, I remember that somehow Dawn became a human bulletin board for the cast. She was the one who knew exactly where each of us was to be during the day, what scenes were going to be shot, and what the schedule for the week entailed. If there were any questions, the remedy was simple: "Ask Dawn." That's the way it was, and she was pretty reliable. We all loved it.

Originally, Dawn did not intend to become an actress. When she was growing up in Reno, Nevada, she took dancing lessons to be a ballerina. Trick knees made her look for something else. At Stephens College in Columbia, Missouri, an all-girls school located smack in the center of the state, Dawn started out as a chemistry major, later leaning toward theater training. When she graduated, her first role was in a play. Dawn portrayed a fourteen-year-old boy, if you can believe that.

In Hollywood, she slid into television roles, and "knock on wood," she says, she has not been out of work since—except by choice. After "Gilligan's," Dawn returned to the theater to "stretch a bit," fearing the same typecasting we all did. Her home base was Nashville for many years, and in 1987 Dawn moved back to the Los Angeles area, where she continues to stay active in theater.

Dawn was the youngest of all the cast, and I think we all had our special friendship with her. She's that type of person. I think late in Natalie Schafer's life Dawn became like a daughter to her. "She became somewhat of a surrogate mother to me. I think I might have

(PERSONALITY PHOTOS, INC.)

Dawn being interviewed at a "Gilligan's Island" charity fund-raiser in Columbia, Missouri, a few years back. (PHOTO BY STEVE COX)

been the daughter she didn't have," Dawn says of their close relationship. "Natalie was a very, very nosy person, and she wanted to know everything about my love life and such. She was the kind of person you could tell anything to because she never judged you." Dawn became Natalie's family in a sense, and the two of them went out together often. Dawn told me about the time they spent a week together in Florida and how people did a double take when they saw Mrs. Howell and Mary Ann walking down the street.

For more than ten years, Dawn has returned to Columbia to cohost an annual telethon that benefits the local children's hospital through the Children's Miracle Network. "I feel we all have a responsibility to this," Dawn says. "I am a firm believer in that. And you get back what you put out. It all comes around. The rewards of seeing these children recover makes it worth it."

A few years ago Dawn began a small business venture called Wishing Wells, which distributes a catalogue featuring a clothing line for people who have difficulty dressing themselves, like arthritis sufferers or the elderly who may be infirm. Dawn laughs when she says she gets letters from people who say, "Oh, I just *knew* Mary Ann would end up doing something nice like that."

$E = mc^2$

~~~~~~

O N E thing people ask me is how close the Professor was to my real personality. Maybe they *believe* the television and assume I really am that island intellectual with an IQ just points away from Einstein's. Those same people may find it amusing to know that I flunked a few subjects in high school and was held back half a year.

My father's death shaped the events in my life for many years. I was eight years old when my father died of pneumonia. In the midst of the Great Depression, my mother was left to raise six kids in Ashley, Pennsylvania. Someone told her about a school in Philadelphia called Girard College that was for "poor white male orphans." It was established in 1850 by Stephen Girard, a Frenchman. Let me point out that many years earlier, the Commonwealth of Pennsylvania characterized any fatherless child as "an orphan."

My mother had the courage to do what she thought was right for us, and in retrospect I have come to realize what a difficult position she was in and what a good job she did. She was a great woman, and I miss her.

A few months after my father's death, my younger brothers, Kenneth and David, and I were enrolled in Girard College, all on the same day. I spent the majority of my youth within those tall stone walls. I lived and I grew up there.

It was pretty hard for an eight-year-old to lose his father, be torn away from his home, separated from his mother, and placed in an institution where he was one of 1,800 boys. There were huge buildings and long rooms with spotless wooden floors and an overwhelming militarized feeling about the whole place. At times, however, there was a lot of warmth.

It took a long time to get used to our sudden uprooting because at Girard we were scared—not only of other guys but of the disciplinarians as well. This fear surfaced when we saw boys getting hit and knocked down and we wondered what was going on—and then came to the realization that sooner or later it could happen to us, so we learned how to play the game, how to get along in a situation like that and survive.

Because my father was working for the Reading Railroad when he died, we could take advantage of free passes. We went back and forth by train from Philadelphia and Ashley (about 125 miles apart) during our vacations: ten days at Christmas and two months in the summer. Even before we could leave, however, my mother had to prove she could support us for the sixty days.

In a lot of ways, I wish my childhood had been different. I wish I had had a father whom I knew. But that didn't happen. I wanted to be closer to my mother, but it was a double-edged situation. I knew I couldn't be. One thing Girard insisted on was that you write a letter every Sunday to your mother. And I did that. If anything, I learned a bit of self-discipline during my childhood. At a very early age, I learned how to hide my feelings, in essence, how to act.

I was flunking algebra when I was a sophomore in high school. Algebra just didn't register with me. I couldn't grasp it. And in those days, if you flunked one subject, you went to summer school. If you flunked two, you went to summer school. Failing three courses meant you were held back for a term, but you could go home for the summer.

I *knew* I was flunking algebra and there was no way to salvage my grades, so I deliberately flunked two other subjects, social studies and, I think, history. I wanted to go home for the summer because summer was escape time and nobody was going to deprive me of that.

Up until that point I was a C and D student. After I was held back, I made a decision that I was not going to be that kind of student anymore. It was a conscious decision that I repeated in my mind. I even said it aloud a few times.

From that point on, I concentrated; I became an A student, and I was elected to the National Honor Society. I was a leader in every way I could be at Girard. I became a captain in the cadet battalion, and I led our unit to a competitive drill championship. I played a decent game at almost any sport, and at that time I formulated an interest in acting.

I don't know whether I dug deep into my life experiences for the role of Professor Roy Hinkley. I was not the smartest in our school, but I remember the guy who was. It's funny how you always remember the advanced one in your class. We had one of those geniuses at Girard. His name was Walter Hartfield, and he was one of sixty-six guys in my class. Believe me, he was the brain all the way through school. And he played the piano exceptionally well; Walter gave many recitals for the rest of the students.

In 1992 I returned to Girard's campus for my fifty-year class reunion. The school is still operating, albeit with changes. Today, it is multiracial and coeducational, and the enrollment is not nearly what it used to be.

A lot of emotions went through me during that trip, and I'm glad my wife was with me to reminisce with old friends. A few even asked me to sign autographs for their grandchildren, and that made me feel terrific. For all of us who grew up in the confines of Girard, there were shared feelings of the whole range of emotions, including respect and love for our school and for our benefactor, Stephen Girard.

I also found out that Walter Hartfield had died, but who knows, maybe a little bit of Walter lives on in the Professor.

FEATURES OF THE
BLACKTOPPED LAGOON

THERE were mornings during the California winter months that chilled the lagoon to a crisp forty degrees and when you jumped in, the shock almost took your breath away. Many times Bob had to wear a wet suit under his jeans and red rugby shirt with the collar buttoned all the way up to conceal it. I wore one, too, but it didn't work well because we weren't moving around in the water that much so it didn't contain much body heat.

Some months the water felt great and we did the shot in the afternoon when it was good and sweltering outside. Natalie would be the first to run in. But some months it was like jumping into a pool of melting ice and you can tell that we hesitated in some scenes. For some reason, the ice water didn't bother Alan, so we used to kid him about being "well insulated."

Poor Bobby. Those lagoon scenes really got to him because he was in that murky water the most, I think. I remember once it was just turning daylight and we were all at the lagoon getting ready to do the outdoor shots before an afternoon storm rolled through Southern California. Bobby had to lay at the bottom of the lagoon with a weight on his chest and wait for "Action" to be called before he would sit up and say his lines for the camera. Take after take, he had to repeat it.

On our show, no man was an island. (COURTESY OF CBS AND SHERWOOD SCHWARTZ)

That ice water was creeping into his wet suit, and he was in the water shivering so long that he couldn't get his lines out. His lips were purple. He couldn't take it any longer, so he just walked up to his dressing room and turned on the shower and stepped in with his clothes on, tennis shoes, cap, everything still on. Steam floated out of Bobby's dressing room and you could hear him let out one of those sighs that go along with a hot, foaming Jacuzzi.

We shot "Gilligan's Island" on CBS's Studio City lot in the Valley, four or five miles away from what is actually Hollywood. The lagoon was on the back lot; everything else—every hut, cave, and dream—was filmed indoors on Soundstage 2 with one camera and no audience. Eventually, the sand on Stage 2 was swept away and that very same floor became the stomping grounds for

Some days, the lagoon was so frigid that we had to wear wet suits under our costumes. (AUTHOR'S COLLECTION)

Mary Tyler Moore and her cast when they filmed her hit show in the early seventies.

When the huts and palm trees occupied Stage 2 for our South Seas sanctuary, a sky-blue cyclorama surrounded the back of the set. We had just a few interchangeable huts that were re-dressed to transform, say, the Howells' hut into Skipper and Gilligan's. I was usually stuck in the supply hut.

There was greenery everywhere—in pots and buckets; some palm trees were tied up with sacks around their bases. Some of our indoor palm trees were held up by planks that were nailed to the floor. An assortment of Styrofoam boulders with flat bottoms were scattered around for decoration. It was a jungle out there.

Wind machines were on the sidelines sometimes, kicking up a little sand now and then. Oh, the sand. It was only about an inch thick on the floor, but every day I took off my shoes in my dressing room and let some sand run out into the trash can before I removed my socks with the stuff caked to the bottom of my socks.

Simulating an uncharted island, the "Gilligan's" pilot was filmed on the island of Kauai in Hawaii; the exact site is Moloa'a Bay. Some of this pilot footage wound up in later episodes intermixed with footage we shot at Zuma Beach, near Malibu in California. After those first few episodes, we never shot on a beach again.

People still ask about the lagoon. I think it took a few inspections and alterations before they got it right, but the CBS greensmen, designers, and contracted landscapers made this lagoon out of a corner chunk of land. Artificial palm trees that were bald of palm fronds were planted around the pool they were digging. Eventually,

Alan and Bob would never have predicted that our show was in for a long haul. (AUTHOR'S COLLECTION)

palm leaves were attached and much more tropical greenery—some live, mostly plastic—was brought in and crowded around the ground area. The pool began looking more like a lake area; then they blacktopped the lagoon's belly, poured water in, and it leaked terribly. So they had to empty the lagoon, fix it, and fill it again.

The lagoon was emptied and refilled a few times when the water got way too scummy to jump in or even to look presentable for Gilligan to pass by and discover a NASA spacecraft or something. The only other interference we experienced while filming at the lagoon was the occasional airplane that rose from the nearby Burbank airport and flew overhead.

The lush lagoon, four feet deep with a working waterfall, cost $75,000. There have been rumors that the lagoon was converted into a parking lot, however. As of this writing, our tropical paradise is still there at CBS.

(Oh, and don't be duped: Your tour guide on the tram at Universal Studios will tell you the lake you are passing was "the lagoon for Gilligan." What they don't say is that it was used only once, in a TV reunion movie.)

For those of you who thought we never actually pinpointed the island on a map, well, here's your answer: You know that wavy shot of the island in the distance just as you're coming back from a commercial? You know, the same island right behind the show's title. That was Coconut Island, one of Hawaii's tiniest.

For those honeymooners who want to visit the most televised island in history, it's located in Kaneohe Bay on the northeast shore of Oahu. The twenty-five-acre island was not uncharted by film crews. It also served as the location for the film *Bird of Paradise*.

Coconut Island came up for sale a few years ago. UPI reported that the owner wanted $8.75 million for the property, which included: an estate home, cabins, a beach cabana, a swimming lagoon, a boathouse, and more. Best suited as a millionaire's retreat, the island was host to such celebrities as Presidents Harry Truman and Lyndon Johnson. Newspapers also reported that ousted Philippine President Ferdinand Marcos visited the island with thoughts of seclusion there.

Did I miss a few episodes?

"THE BALLAD OF GILLIGAN'S ISLAND"

~~~~~~~~~~~~~~~~~~~~~~~~~~~~~~

I<small>T'S</small> probably true that more kids can recall the lyrics to the "Gilligan's Island" theme song than can recite our country's Pledge of Allegiance.

It's also probable that our show's opening theme song is the most famous of all TV theme songs. And yet, when "Gilligan's Island" was still under construction, the tune as we know it was not the first choice. In fact, it was out of sheer, painful desperation that the song came about at all.

Sherwood Schwartz, who fully subscribed to that "necessity is the mother of invention" rule, sat right back and wrote the theme with a friend of his—only after receiving the devastating news that the network detested "Gilligan's Island" and refused to put it on the air. You see, although the network had firmly rejected Sherwood's original pilot film for a shipwreck series, Sherwood was confident that with some alterations and editing, CBS would reconsider. And he knew that the show's opening was an elemental constituent in understanding the program's concept.

While Sherwood was frantically retooling his pilot film for the network, he decided to replace the original calypso theme, which was sung by one vocalist. It had a tropical feel to it, but it was "more indigenous to the Caribbean," he says. Sherwood and his friend, composer George Wyle, penned a new opening, whose purpose was not to be catchy or amusing or an attempt to top the charts. The opening song was written specifically to introduce the characters and explain, in capsule form, the shipwreck of the S.S. *Minnow*. In doing so, Sherwood successfully followed the same strategy employed by other situation comedies of the day, like the storytelling "Ballad of Jed Clampett" from "The Beverly Hillbillies."

Gilligan's sixty-second ballad came about in a mad dash to complete the lyrics and melody, record it with a group of professional singers, and edit the whole thing with the pilot's film footage. It all had to be accomplished in time to screen the final print for network executives in New York. Because the song had to be recorded on a weekend and there were no recording studios available, Sherwood begged favors from friends to get it done in a couple of days. He hadn't even found a group to sing it yet.

Finally, through Wyle, a group of hungry but very talented folksingers who were making a name for themselves around Hollywood were chosen to record the theme. This was accomplished on a Sunday afternoon in a makeshift studio that had been quickly set up

The men on the island formed a rock group called the Gnats.
(RUSSELL JOHNSON COLLECTION)

in a garage at the home of Sherwood's friend, writer-producer Mel Shavelson. While recording was going on, a dinner party was in preparation in the house. Just before the singers were ready for a take, someone would whistle and the clattering of dishes and plates all stopped. The hired waiters all had to freeze.

With Sherwood's determination and luck, the track was recorded, albeit it was as primitive as could be. Barely making the deadline, the tape was cut together with the film and an "answer print" for the new pilot was flown to New York for another screening by the brass. This time, they loved it!

Strangely, until now not much has been known about the three young, clean-cut folksingers who harmonized the vocals and played their guitars for our theme song that afternoon in a garage. They were a trio known as the Wellingtons, college buddies all in their early twenties who came from the University of Illinois. Their names were George Patterson, Kirby Johnson, and Ed Wade.

Over the years, Sherwood had lost contact with them, and these guys seemed to have slipped into obscurity. As it turns out, they had eagerly ventured into the music industry in the early sixties, broken up in the late sixties, and, after becoming like brothers over the years, gone their separate ways. George Patterson attended the University of Southern California and became a respected psychologist; Ed Wade became a successful attorney and is now a partner in a large law firm; and Kirby Johnson stayed in the music business, arranging for the likes of Arlo Guthrie, Ike and Tina Turner, Carly Simon, and Blood, Sweat and Tears. "And I'm the one who's broke," he says with a laugh.

During their decade as professional singers struggling for that hit, there were several times when huge success was dangled in their path, but fate seemed to snatch it away each time. For instance, the group recorded many songs on the Capitol label, but they were "shelved," says Kirby Johnson, "because we sounded too much like the Lettermen." On Capitol they recorded "The Girl from Ipanema" before Astrud Gilberto sang her famous version, but because the songs were shelved, the boys didn't even get a chance with that one. Even with "Gilligan's Island," their bonanza somehow escaped them.

When these folksingers crowded next to the microphones with their guitars and sang about some Skipper and a millionaire, they had the same attitude as most of us involved with the show. They had little faith in the silly song they were singing and much less in the show it was describing. "I didn't particularly like the song," says Kirby Johnson, "because the chord sequence was the same back-and-forth thing that a lot of folk music at the time had. It had a dumb chord progression. A billion songs were written on that." Neverthe-less, none of them knew that what they recorded that afternoon was to become their most famous work—a tune more recognized than most of Elvis's hits.

The Wellingtons, who were competent writers as well as musi-cians, performed under different names during the sixties. At one time they were known as the Continentals; later they became the Lincolns because they came from Champaign, Illinois. These col-lege buddies had decided to break into the music profession and try to hit it big at a time when folksinging was popular. The Kingston Trio and the Brothers Four were doing pretty well, so they thought it was time to hit the West Coast and see what they could do.

Before the guys settled on naming themselves the Wellingtons—which had a British ring to it—they subjected themselves to a "Name-the-Group" contest on TV's "Jukebox Saturday Night." At that time they were a quartet (the fourth member was Rick Girard, who left to produce Jefferson Airplane's first album). They consid-ered hundreds of suggestions, such as "Sons of the Beaches" and "The Four Maldehydes." They even turned down one man's list of simple kitchen utensils: "The Blenders," "The Spoons," "The Win-dows," and get this—"The Doors."

Their first professional recording was a version of "On Top of Old Smoky," which was included on an album by Roger Williams. Walt Disney became an integral part of the group's exposure when they performed at the Disneyland Hotel. The cartoon mogul was sitting in the front row at one of their live performances and signed them for his record label. They sang the sound-track title song for the Disney film *Savage Sam* and recorded with Annette Funicello for Disney-land Records. For that label they also recorded "The Ballad of Davy Crockett" and "The Wonderful World of Color."

Just sittin' right back: George Patterson, Kirby Johnson, and Ed Wade were the young folksingers known as The Wellingtons who sang our theme song. (COURTESY OF KIRBY JOHNSON)

Later on, the Wellingtons became a regular backup group on the ABC-TV rock 'n' roll show "Shindig," which hosted every big name in the business back then, including the Righteous Brothers, the Beach Boys, and the Beatles. Later, the Wellingtons toured with Donald O'Connor's act, which opened more doors for the group, but still, these Midwestern boys never reached the level of success they had dreamed of when they were on the road struggling to find gigs and playing conventions, music festivals, and the resorts in Estes Park, Colorado.

When the Wellingtons were approached about singing the theme song to "Gilligan's Island," they thought it would be fun, and they shared enthusiasm about getting further television exposure, but it wasn't something they thought would last. Unfortunately, for the second season of "Gilligan's Island," the Wellingtons were replaced by another clean-sounding vocal group, the Eligibles, who sounded a lot like them. The new group rerecorded the theme song to eliminate "and the rest" and inserted an important addition to the lyrics: "the Professor an' Mary Ann."

Needless to say, Dawn and I felt we deserved that change in lyrics when it happened, but even more, it meant that our names and faces would be featured in the ship's wheel in the show's opening. But I'm not sure that any of us in the cast noticed that an entirely different music group rerecorded the theme song. Today, none of the former Wellingtons knows positively why he was replaced.

"I don't think any of us were aware of what the considerations were that caused them to redo the theme song," says Ed Wade.

George Patterson is probably the most nostalgic of the former group. He had to think a moment, but he hazily recalled that they might have been approached about rerecording a cleaner, lyrically revised version of the "Gilligan's" theme for the second season's opening, but they were busy working with Donald O'Connor in Las Vegas at the time.

Patterson notes: "I think we were disappointed, but we never said anything to the producers or questioned why we weren't the ones to rerecord the song. And that probably says it best about us as a group. Instead of crawling over everybody, making it at any cost, we were pretty much easygoing about things. Maybe we should have spoken up, but we were too passive about it. And we didn't care, either. We never thought this song would last, and we never thought the show would last. We had a full plate at the time, and we were in pretty good shape."

Patterson vividly recalls the day the fellows were approached with the idea of releasing the "Gilligan's Island" theme as a single because the show was doing so well. "We thought it was a stupid idea," he says. "Who could have known?"

The Wellingtons were linked to our show for two reasons: They recorded the original theme song and they guest-starred as the Mosquitoes, a rock group that landed on the island in "Don't Bug the Mosquitoes." That's where we finally met the guys who sang our theme song.

"DON'T BUG THE MOSQUITOES"

I don't remember a lot from this episode except that Alan, Jim, and I had to get into these ridiculous costumes. We had wigs, wore tights and bright shirts and played these bamboo guitars. Bob was on drums. And Alan was in tights, which was hilarious. That was a sight because he was such a big guy. Every once in a while, the writers gave us a script that had Alan dressed in long underwear, or a grass skirt, or a toga. On him it was especially funny. And he laughed right along with us.

This time, our rescue was ruined by our own ingenuity—not completely Gilligan's fault, either. Here's how it went: The Mosquitoes (Bingo, Bango, Bongo, and Irving), America's hot new rock group, landed on the island for some R and R and to escape from their crazed fans. The Castaways were so desperate to get back to civilization that they schemed to annoy the four singers so much that they would want to return to the mainland. That didn't work. So someone got the brilliant idea of assembling Mr. Howell, the Skipper, and me as a new rock group on the island. And that didn't work. Now Ginger had the girls form a group called the Honeybees and do a number in matching go-go pants and boots. They sang a terrific song called "You Need Us" ("Like a clam needs a shell . . . Like a prisoner needs a cell"). The Honeybees ended up being *too* good, and their talent threatened the Mosquitoes, who fled the island—without us, of course.

The song that we island men sang was indiscernible gobble-dygook, but the women's song wasn't bad at all. A lot of fans ask about this episode because it's so offbeat. Kirby Johnson (who played Irving, with the little dark John Lennon glasses) remembers that Dawn's voice was dubbed by singer-songwriter Carol Connor.

"What I remember most about that episode was the scene in the

The Honeybees. (COURTESY OF GIGI SCHAEFER NAPLES)

hut," Kirby says. "I was lying in a hammock, and we were disturbed by everyone who kept coming in the hut. I had to fall from the hammock onto the hard ground and then jump out of the window. We kept having to do it over and over because Tina Louise kept complaining that she wasn't staged right. She'd say, 'Oh, you've got the wrong side of my face this time.' And after something like twelve takes, I was wondering if I should get stunt pay."

Ed Wade played Bongo. "Doing that episode was a fascinating process," he says. "It was a whole week. It amazed me how much work goes into doing one of those things. What dedication people have to do this, week-in, week-out, and still maintain the enthusiasm. Being around [the cast] was an obvious thrill. And now my daughters love it. They're both aware of it, but especially my eleven-year-old, she thinks it's the greatest thing in the world."

George Patterson (Bango) was the tallest of the group, and actor Les Brown, Jr., who was not one of the Wellingtons, played the fourth Mosquito, Bingo. Patterson recalls working on the set:

> Bob Denver was a low-key, courteous, very professional, and yet soft-spoken, almost shy person, but very pleasant. That surprised me a little bit. We all loved Dawn Wells. She was so pert and down-to-earth and friendly. Tina Louise, well, there wasn't anybody on the show that was stuck on themselves—with one exception. Tina just seemed like typecasting if I ever saw it. A little prima donna, and I don't mean that in a malicious way. That's something I remember very well.
>
> It was ironic, in the episode we were in, we were not singing the theme song. And I remember this: I remember signing the contracts and reading something about seven reruns. I thought, "Are you kidding me? This show?"

The Wellingtons' contract for the original version of the theme song did not provide them with the benefits of everlasting reruns. Ironically, however, twenty years after the three fellows appeared as the Mosquitoes in that one episode, Kirby Johnson took a wild shot and called BMI, the music union, just to inquire if there were any piddling residuals remaining. He couldn't believe it when the lady on the telephone told him of the tidy sum that had built up over the years as remuneration for the two songs the group had written and performed as the Mosquitoes. The checks were just sitting there, waiting to be claimed. "The union didn't know how to reach us," Kirby remembers.

GILLISECOND
(*gill ih sek' und*)

n. The special moment in television history when the "Gilligan's Island" theme song changed from ". . . and the rest" to ". . . the Professor and Mary Ann."

ABOUT THE PROFESSOR

Name: Dr. Roy Hinkley
Birthplace: Cleveland, Ohio
Education: Six degrees in all, including a B.A. from USC, a B.S. from UCLA, an M.A. from SMU, and a Ph.D. from TCU (all achieved in 25 years).
Area(s) of Expertise: medicine; dentistry; biology; agriculture; astronomy; marine biology; geology; anthropology; botany; psychology; physics; law; zoology; chess.
Occupation(s):   Professor and high school science teacher; noted Boy Scout leader (he was the youngest Eagle Scout in Cleveland), and writer.
Reason for taking three-hour tour: To write his book, *Fun with Ferns*.

- From writer David Marc:

  "The Professor is Scientia, the competent voice of empirical reason crying out among the otherwise foolish, inane, and inept."

- From creator Sherwood Schwartz's "bible" of the characters:

  "Very often the Professor is the one who prevents the rest of the group from taking rash actions. The others look to him and his great store of scientific knowledge, especially as it might affect their possibility of rescue. And it is to this end that the Professor dedicates himself."

- From Joey Green's *The Unofficial Gilligan's Island Handbook*:

  "While the Professor may not have a poetic personality, he always seems to have the most sensible solutions. He's actually the only levelheaded person on the island, a bookworm who rarely displays his emotions—in short, a shipwrecked Spock.

(PHOTO BY GABI RONA)

He is clearly the castaways' guiding light and silent leader. He prefers to sit quietly in the background and let the others think that Skipper runs the island. But when it comes to judicial affairs, life-threatening matters, or possible rescue attempts, the Professor unobtrusively assumes leadership.''

THE S.S. *MINNOW*

No one can say "Gilligan's Island" was without hidden meanings. I was surprised to find out recently from Sherwood Schwartz that our shipwrecked vessel, the S.S. *Minnow*, was actually named for someone. It was so christened in dubious honor of the man who, Sherwood insists, "ruined television."

Newton N. Minow was the chairman of the Federal Communications Commission in 1961 when he delivered a now famous speech at a broadcasters' convention lambasting television. He was speaking for the government, and he vehemently denounced our most powerful communications medium as "America's vast wasteland." Gilligan should be proud he had nothing to do with it; we hadn't yet set sail on television.

The result of Minow's speech was "disastrous," Sherwood says. "Until his speech, the networks were conduits and they had no control of programming. Sponsors had more power, and the creative people who created the shows had more authority. Minow gave networks authority and placed the power of programming in the hands of three network heads, who, for a long time, controlled everything coming into your living room. They eventually became the de facto producers of all prime-time programs by having creative control over writing, casting, and directing."

By the time Sherwood started "Gilligan's Island," the networks had just begun to use the dictatorial powers Minow had handed them. "They had an Uzi in their hands," Sherwood says.

I don't think Newton Minow knows about his inadvertent inspiration. Maybe it's better that way. Otherwise, he'd be reminded of it "four times a day in some cities."

Newton Minow, shown here being interviewed by Walter Cronkite in 1962, was the namesake for our boat. In a famous speech, he labeled television "America's vast wasteland." (PERSONALITY PHOTOS, INC.)

REAL LIFE ON THE ISLAND

~~~~~~

WHEN things got a little tough or tense while we were shooting "Gilligan's Island," Alan Hale and I sometimes edged our way clear of any flying fists and we sat and chatted. He used to say to me, "You and I are the guys who hold this thing together, you know that?" This was particularly true in the beginning, when all seven of us were testing the waters with each other, exploring each other's eccentricities and looking out for each other's mood swings. We'd figure out just what button to push to make each other laugh, and we pushed it when things got uptight.

None of us will deny that there was genuine human survival between the actors on this island. Especially at first. Tina Louise was extremely unhappy. Jim Backus and Natalie Schafer were not too happy with it all. It wasn't all-out warfare, but initially things did not go well with any of us. But looking at our show, you would have never known it.

Here is the reason Sherwood Schwartz fought so strongly to preserve his concept of this television show and why his tenacity kept it afloat: If these seven people were forced to survive and their existence was chronicled complete with unadulterated human nature, Gilligan would have surely been cleverly murdered by one of us in the fourth episode and none of us would have been able to figure out who did it. Dissension, paranoia, and anarchy would have been our downfall. End of first season. End of series?

Television portrayed this island survival as a simple, comedic, fun, fast-moving cartoon adventure in which the worst that could happen was that Gilligan would screw up the rescue one more time. Next week, someone new would visit the island, or maybe we'd have to eat soap to save us from the dangerous levels of radiation that tainted our food.

There was no downtime on this island, and that might have been the trick that hooked kids. Our show looked like no other tropical paradise on television, especially in color. And our show moved along at a fast pace, with no dull stretches. I think some kids even thought it would have been wonderful to really be on that island with this crew of crazy people, always throwing parties and putting on plays and such. Some fans have told me that after school they went out and played "Gilligan's Island" instead of playing "house" or other games. So life on the island really wasn't so bad. No taxes. No

Dawn just cracked me up with something. (© 1993 CBS, INC.)

Right Castaways, wrong radio. (PHOTO BY GABI RONA)

pollution. No money problems. But, of course, no bathrooms, so the place was far from perfect.

Sherwood was right: Anything other than completely incongruous fantasy would have been too gruesome to swallow.

Unfortunately, real life in this televised jungle was not as ridiculously happy as it looked—especially during the first ten weeks of filming. Sherwood Schwartz recalls that turbulent period as "grim." It was a difficult time that most of us would probably like to forget.

Dawn Wells, Alan Hale, and I were more even-tempered than the rest, at least at work. Don't get me wrong, however; there were "days" for all of us. Jim Backus could be irascible, and you just knew when to leave him alone. Natalie Schafer was not too keen on the show from the beginning. She didn't know what she had gotten into. I really don't think any of us did. And certainly Tina Louise didn't.

Natalie wouldn't pull any punches. She'd say, "You know, I've done films, and I've done theater, and I've done Broadway . . . and here I am doing this crap." There were days when I had the same attitude. We might have all been guilty of the same notion when we began the series, but eventually the waters calmed. In time, we became a strong union, and, as an ensemble, we pulled it off.

I have to give credit to our director, John Rich, who got us through those first thirteen weeks; that unlucky number of weeks is the standard network trial period for a new show that's been placed on the air. Rich took charge and didn't take any temperament from Tina, or from any of us, for that matter. He knew what he wanted, and he knew how to get it out of us for the camera.

We all realized this, and, for the most part, I think we all admired him for it. I know I did. If we had had almost any other director, our

Tina and Janos Prohaska, the stuntman who played most of the gorillas on our show. (COURTESY OF SHERWOOD SCHWARTZ)

cast would have self-destructed. We couldn't have done better than John Rich, who had directed "The Dick Van Dyke Show," "Bonanza," and many other shows. After ours, he directed some fantastic episodes of "All in the Family."

When we were in production, we took the show seriously. The funniest comedy has to be taken seriously, and it's always carefully orchestrated.

Generally, the cast came in on Monday, at 10:00 A.M. or so, for a cold reading. At that time we took care of any special wardrobe needs, which left Bob, Alan, and me with plenty of free time. I loved that. I never changed my clothes, it seemed.

I hated movies about changing clothes. Years ago, working on films while under contract to Universal Studios, I used to hope the role would be one in which I wore the same thing forever. And with "Gilligan's Island," I got it.

My costume was simple: I had a rack of several pairs of khaki pants, several light-blue oxford shirts, and yellow socks with a ring around the top. On occasion, like for a Howell cotillion, wardrobe would dress the Professor up a little bit with a brown corduroy sport jacket. Those dark-blue "boat shoes" that Bob, Alan, Jim, and I wore have now become famous in America as a style of tennis shoe. Those K Mart specials are high fashion now.

If it was a "dream week," though—one of those weeks in which we did an episode featuring a dream sequence—we had to be fitted for some outlandish costume that only accented the ridiculousness of it all. Usually, that also meant that some or all of us would have to meet specially with our makeup man, Keester Sweeney, to devise a way to reshape our appearances to accommodate the script.

From Tuesday through Friday, we filmed the show, always "out of sequence," the way a motion picture is shot. For instance, one morning we might begin with a scene in which the Castaways rush out to the lagoon only to realize that the dirty dog who visited our island has left us there to rot. We'd chase Gilligan into the water, and the final scene of the show was "in the can." This was done while the sun was bright enough for shooting, and no planes or jets from

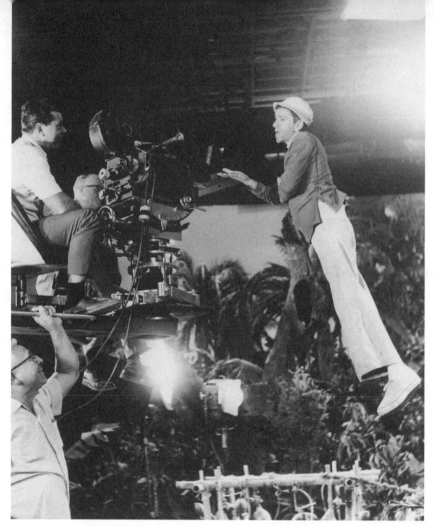

It seemed as if every other script called for Bobby to be strung up by a wire.
(AUTHOR'S COLLECTION)

the nearby Lockheed plant or the Burbank airport caused any disruption.

On another afternoon, we might be on the soundstage doing the final scene of another episode. It might be a night scene with tiki torches lit all around the darkened stage. Inside the studio, daylight and outside weather conditions made no difference.

When we were not filming, we usually had our studio chairs gathered around together on the side of the set. Some of us had the small folding studio chairs, and some of us had the tall kind. Relaxing together, we listened to Jim and Alan tell jokes unendingly,

A disaster waiting to happen. (© 1993 CBS, INC.)

never repeating the same one. If there was anyone I could count on to give me a good laugh at work, it was Alan and Jim.

Tina rarely joined us. Mostly, she went off to the side by herself or back to her dressing room, preferring not to socialize. And Bob, who is more naturally introverted, joined us when he was in a "community" mood, or when he had a chance. He was in the majority of the shots in each episode and had more lines to memorize than the rest of us, so he was constantly busy.

Because the work could be fatiguing, Bob wanted to keep things moving, and he got really upset at what he felt was unnecessary delay. Occasionally, he and Tina got into an argument, and Sherwood had to leave his office and come down onto the set and try to cool things off so work could continue.

Bob explains it like this:

I just think it was a matter that she didn't quite know what she was doing when filming a series. She was holding up shooting a lot. We were all working late hours, and that's unfair to everybody. Whether she was justified in holding everybody up or not, I don't care. The hair and makeup shouldn't take that long. That was my complaint. But we settled it and from then on, things were fine.

Unlike most half-hour sitcoms shot on videotape today, we needed four days to film our show. Many current sitcoms are blocked and the script is rewritten over the course of four days. On the last day it's finally shot in an afternoon or an evening in front of an audience.

It took us those four full, exhausting days to complete each episode because there were many special effects involved, and even

Beauty and the beast.
(PERSONALITY
PHOTOS, INC.)

Ida Lupino (bottom) was one of our directors. Visiting the set are friends of Alan Hale's (clockwise, from left): Mrs. James Valk, Bob, Alan, James Valk, Trinket Hale (Alan's wife), and Alan's stand-in, Tom Keegan. Tom was the longtime stand-in for Alan's father in many motion pictures. (COURTESY OF MRS. ALAN HALE, JR.)

though the crews who pulled them off were some of the most efficient craftsmen I've ever seen, it all took an incredible amount of time. Remember, this was not simply a living-room-and-kitchen sitcom. We had many different shots to set up in every show. Back and forth from the hut to a cave, to the lagoon, and back to the hammocks. No two caves looked alike on our island. That pace kept the show moving, and it kept us moving.

We might shoot from 8:00 A.M. until 12:30 and break for an hour lunch, or, if we were running behind, we just snacked for a half hour right there on the set. At least one day out of each show, the cast and crew got together and feasted on an Italian spread that made us all go nuts just inhaling it before lunchtime. The whole studio smelled of garlic.

There was an Italian fellow who worked as a craft-service guy on the set. (Craft-service is the common term on any television or film set for the organization that supplies the food and arranges a spread of edibles to munch on during breaks or just while you're waiting to be called.) At any given time, there might be an overstuffed banquet of chips, pretzels, dips, spreads, cheeses, fruit, sandwiches, sodas, and always coffee.

Behind the cyclorama with the painted sky on it, this craft-service guy had two oven ranges lit up full force, and he arranged long tables full of Italian foods, with breads and wines. I think Alan, who loved to cook and eat, really looked forward to those feasts. This is how he remembered them:

> The craft guy had one stove and an icebox, so I brought in another stove and an icebox to the set and the boys on the crew came in on their own time to start those cauldrons of food. With an open set, I remember we'd invite everybody on the lot to our set for a luncheon. We had some marvelous guests. Big Jim Arness from "Gunsmoke" would drop by for lunch. We had Bette Davis and Jean Arthur.
>
> Dear Jean Arthur, the marvelous actress, was somewhat like a startled fawn. She didn't really make contact with anybody on her own set, but she did come over and have lunch with us. All through filming, the garlic was flowing through the set. Everybody from the other shows would come over.

The cuisine wasn't always Italian. A lot of guys on the crew were fishermen. If word got around the set on Monday that the weekend had provided a big catch for one of them, we knew the seafood was going to be good and fresh. Everybody pitched in a buck to take care of expenses and the birthdays that rolled around.

THE *TV GUIDE* SHOOT

There have been rumors over the years that have described Bob Denver as a monster for refusing to pose for publicity pictures with a temperamental Tina Louise. It's true that Tina got quite a bit of press because of her natural beauty, which unquestionably sells in print media. But that rumor has been stretched a bit over time. Here is what actually happened:

TV Guide wanted to photograph Bob and Tina, possibly attempting to add some romantic undertone to the show—which was the furthest idea from the show's premise. Bob refused to model for the photographer unless Dawn Wells was included in the shot. "After all, I was working with both girls every day and I wanted it to be fair," Bob explains.

The editors at *TV Guide* agreed to Bob's request, except when they shot the photos, they mysteriously instructed Dawn to remove all of her makeup, she says. Dawn did it because that's what the photographer wanted, but she thought it was strange at the time. When the cover appeared on the stands a few weeks later, Dawn had been completely cropped out of the photo—except for a small portion of one pigtail that you can see at the edge of the magazine's stapled spine.

"Needless to say, *TV Guide* is not my favorite magazine," Bob says.

(REPRINTED WITH PERMISSION FROM *TV GUIDE*® MAGAZINE. COPYRIGHT 1965, 1966 BY NEWS AMERICA PUBLICATIONS, INC.)

Golf pro Al Besselink visits his friend Jim Backus on the set of "The Big Gold Strike" in December 1964. Bob Denver caddies. (PERSONALITY PHOTOS, INC.)

DRIVE, HE SAID

Alan and Jim were incessant golfers. These guys took this hobby so seriously, there were mornings when they'd shoot nine holes before they came into the studio at 7:00 to begin filming. I'm not sure about Jim, but I know that Alan was a long-time member of The Hollywood Hackers, a golf club with a stellar membership that included nearly every big name in town. Trinket, Alan's wife, said that after he died, she had no idea what to do with the more than twenty sets of golf clubs that sat in the garage.

One day during a break in filming, Alan and Jim headed out to the CBS back lot behind the lagoon and decided to finally settle an argument about who could drive a ball farther. Both of them shot yards away into a ravine and neither of them felt like strutting way over there to prove who was champ, so they just kept up their funny battle. "My ball went at least ten yards farther than yours," Alan shouted.

"Nonsense!" Jim yelled back.

Then the studio guard caught up with Jim and Alan. One of them had driven a ball right into some guy's windshield in the parking lot.

Jim immediately poked his club into Alan's stomach and said, "He outdrove me by a mile!"

NATALIE SAVES HER KEESTER

~~~~~~

WE had a makeup man on the show who had worked at MGM for years. He specialized in women's makeup, but this guy was an expert at making anyone look better than he or she really did. His name was Keester Sweeney, and the reason he was placed on our show is that Natalie Schafer, who had worked with him at MGM, insisted on bringing him along. And thank God she did.

Keester was one of the best makeup artists in Hollywood, and his career went back to the golden age of filmmaking. He taught many of the best makeup artists in film and television today, but he never had the desire to head up a studio makeup department. It didn't interest him at all. Keester became part of our family, and even after his retirement in the 1970s he rejoined us for a couple of the television movies. I'm sure Natalie had a hand in that, too, and Keester loved it. Our whole cast loved his perfectly accurate adjustments and alterations.

Keester made me look better than anybody ever has. He showed me all kinds of tricks, and after "Gilligan's" I realized he had spoiled me. My eyelids, for instance. They are the heavy type that sink a bit. And my eyebrows are light in color and fade out at the temples. Keester filled in my eyebrows and stretched my brow a bit to open my eyes up. Keester also had a way of shadowing my nose and hiding my double chin subtly, so I looked better on TV than I did anywhere else. Whenever another makeup person attended to me because of time restraints, I always went back to Keester and asked him to fix their work.

Naturally, the girls loved him. Especially Natalie. We didn't know it then, but she was well near seventy years old when we were doing the show. None of us realized that until after she died because she always looked good. She gave much of the credit to ol' Keester.

(PHOTO BY GABI RONA.)

*   *   *

Keester loved his craft and said he looked forward to coming to work each day on our show. He was there bright and early with the women, getting them ready long before the guys because they generally required more time. Keester performed his magic on them, then they emerged for the cameras—but not until they were absolutely perfect.

I used to kid Dawn, "They don't make you up, they assemble you." Dawn kept a secret from the viewers during the show: Just

Little Lovey, Natalie, and Tongo (Denny Miller) on their way to the soundstage. (© 1993 CBS, INC.)

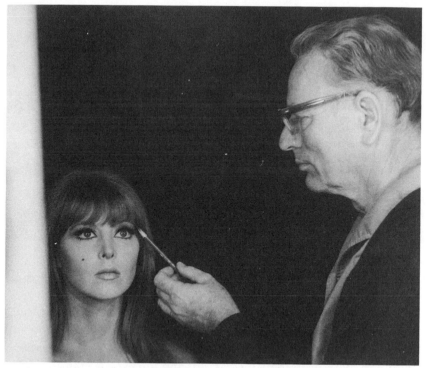

In this snapshot aimed into the mirror, our makeup man Keester Sweeney puts the finishing touches on Tina Louise. (AUTHOR'S COLLECTION)

before shooting she inserted tiny tooth caps in her mouth. She kept the two little caps in a small vial that she carried around, and she snapped them on right next to her two front teeth. Voila! Her smile was pearly and perfect.

The caps attached easily to her real teeth, which happen to be just a smidgen shorter than the others, making her smile "a bit bucky," as she said. Any time Dawn ate in a scene, she either didn't have the caps in or she pretended to chew food. The "defect" was hardly noticeable, but just enough so that Dawn had these snap-ons fitted. The only time Dawn removed those babies for the camera was in a few dream sequences, when it took every bit of ammunition possible to make her look ugly. And certainly Dawn was beautiful then, and, personally, I think she's more beautiful now—if that's possible.

HAIRY COCONUTS AND
BAMBOO SHOOTS

~~~~~~~~~~~~~~~~~~~~~~~~~~~~~~~~~~~~~

OU R prop department made fantastic things. I wish I had some of them now, like those plastic coconuts we drank from or my makeshift laboratory setup constructed of intricate pieces of bamboo and vines, with dripping island serum and little Bunsen burners and test gourds.

We used to cheer the prop guys when we came on the set and saw how they had accomplished the script's needs. One time the story called for a primitive little car for Gilligan to chauffeur the lazy Howells around in. The crew just couldn't wait for us to try it out; they were like the kid on Christmas who can't wait for his dad to finish assembling his bike. They had made this little auto look like a Yugo, and each of us wanted to get in it and drive it around. (Eventually, Gilligan ran it into the lagoon and it sank.)

Of course, the propmen and the special effects guys were efficient and tested every contraption and explosion well ahead of the shooting day. At any given time Sherwood had more than ten scripts stacked on his desk just waiting to be produced, so the crews had time to perfect their inventions. They rarely screwed up for the camera, and usually everyone on the set applauded them.

These guys loved their work because it brought out their creativity. Generally speaking, in a studio prop shop, you're not making

a lot of things, you're ordering stuff from large prop houses. But for "Gilligan's" they had a distinct assignment: They had to solve a problem and do it with bamboo, gourds, strands of rope, and coconut shells.

At first, the prop guys gave us real coconut halves to drink from. The only problem was that these hairy coconuts became soft and began to leak under the studio's hot lights. You can see them sweating, if you look closely, in the first season's episodes.

Plus, everything on the island had to appear to be assembled badly. For instance, those huts were supposed to be made by seven people who really didn't know what they were doing. (Six, anyway.) The crew would show off something they had constructed and Sherwood would politely say, "No, no. This needs to be *worse*. The

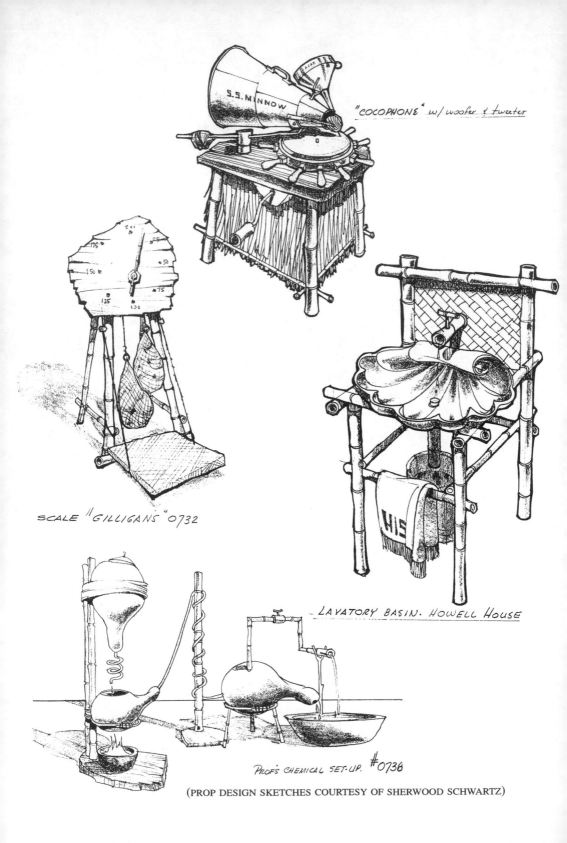

"COCOPHONE" w/ woofer & tweeter

SCALE "GILLIGANS" 0732

LAVATORY BASIN. HOWELL HOUSE

PROF'S CHEMICAL SET-UP. #0736

(PROP DESIGN SKETCHES COURTESY OF SHERWOOD SCHWARTZ)

This was Alan: One minute you're delivering your line, and the next minute he's standing on your foot so you can't exit the scene. (COURTESY OF SHERWOOD SCHWARTZ)

bamboo supports need to be more like *six* inches off line." Then, all was perfect. There's a perfectionist in that Schwartz fellow.

It got to the point where the whole "Gilligan's" company looked forward to seeing how these ingenious crew members would build Mr. Howell's pool table or a bicycle-driven washing machine for Mary Ann. The crew would usually explain how the contraptions worked to me because I had to explain it to the Castaways and turn the switch on.

The whole soundstage would often be full of visitors who were curious because they had heard around the lot that we had a doozy: some kind of monstrous, four-man, pedal-powered bamboo carnival ride that produced electricity when we rode around on it.

THE PROFESSOR'S ISLAND INVENTIONS

Okay, okay, so I couldn't build a boat. The Professor improvised with gadgets and concocted some pretty wild antidotes, but I must refute something. Despite what you hear, the Professor *never* built a nuclear reactor or a satellite communications system out of clamshells. Here's an inventory of what he did build:

- a bamboo lie detector (hooked up to the ship's horn and the radio's batteries)
- shark repellent
- a coconut-shell battery recharger
- a bamboo telescope
- jet-pack fuel
- a strychnine serum that temporarily paralyzes Gilligan
- keptibora-berry extract to remedy Gilligan's double vision
- a helium balloon (rubber raincoats sewn together and sealed with tree sap)
- a bamboo xylophone
- soap made from plant fats
- a Geiger counter
- lead radiation suits and makeup (protection from a meteor's cosmic rays)
- a pedal-powered bamboo sewing machine
- an electrode linked to a pedal-powered generator
- a washing machine, water pump, and telegraph, all pedal-powered
- an assortment of hair tonics, antiseptics, poisons, "spider cider" (to kill off a gargantuan black morning spider), and even a batch of nitroglycerine
- Mr. Howell's roulette wheel and pool table

JUNGLE BLUNDERS

~~~~~~

FOR some strange reason, fans have a fixation about accidents that occurred while we were filming the show. There is something about physical harm and catastrophic misfortunes that stimulates the imagination and heightens curiosity. It's human nature, like slowing down to gawk at a twisted wreck on the highway.

Truthfully, none of us ever suffered any serious injuries while filming "Gilligan's." Really. Every one of us was in every single episode, and, luckily, not one of us missed a show.

The mishaps, which emerged from simple slapstick gone awry, sometimes meant a whirl to the emergency room or a rewrite of the script. And other times, there were close calls. For instance, fate was on Bob Denver's side the time Gilligan and Skipper switched hammocks for a scene. I don't recall why Skipper was in the top hammock, but it was part of the script.

In rehearsal one day, Alan Hale—who was every pound as solid as he looked—made a free-fall from the top hammock right down onto a mat on the sandy floor. You could hear him yell "Dooop!" from across the stage.

All of a sudden, Bob looked out from the bottom hammock, white as a ghost. He stared and took a breath. He had been lying there quietly preparing to drop out of his hammock first, and if Alan had plummeted onto him, a few of Bob's skinny bones would have snapped.

You can guess the rest: The Professor would have had to make a cast for Gilligan to wear conspicuously for many episodes.

In one show, if you look closely, you can see a bandage on Alan's right ear. In this episode we put on a play and Ginger and Mrs. Howell argued about who would play Cleopatra. Near the end, Gilligan carried a bamboo ladder onstage and Skipper (dressed in undershorts and a toga) walked right through it, breaking the rungs. The propmen demonstrated the gag for Alan, and the thin bamboo they had made for the rungs snapped as easily as pretzels. Alan tried the gag once, and when the soft bamboo broke, it exposed a sharp edge that sliced into his ear.

Even though a bandage covered the laceration on the top half of his ear, on film it was almost completely hidden with makeup. Our director merely moved the camera angle back a bit and changed the shot from closeup to medium. Right afterward, we all went back to work.

Alan's dedication to the show was undaunted. He would do just about anything to assist in its health. This is a guy who took a fall from a palm tree and broke his wrist but told no one. There were two more episodes to film that season before we scattered on hiatus, and Alan didn't want to disturb the course of events. He never took a day off and never complained.

At our wrap party celebrating the close of the first season, Sherwood Schwartz took Alan aside and asked him why his wrist looked painfully swollen. Alan told him about the accident. None of us knew until then. When Alan finally went to his doctor, he was fitted with a cast from wrist to elbow.

Alan's wife, Trinket, laughs about it now, but she recalls that they had attended the Kentucky Derby celebration just a few days after Alan got his cast. In their hotel room one night, Trinket was just getting to sleep when Alan unknowingly swung his arm and conked her on the head with his cast.

But Alan wasn't the only trouper. Jim Backus, in his own way, was a stoic. Sherwood got a call at home from him one night. Jim said he was in agony, but he'd be all right to show up for work the next day.

Alan has just had his right ear accidentally ripped open by a bamboo pole. If you look closely you can see the bandage. (COURTESY OF MRS. ALAN HALE, JR.)

He wanted Sherwood to change the script so he could sit in a scene rather than move about. It seems ol' Jim was carrying a tube of Preparation H in his satchel that week, so Sherwood simply had Mr. Howell and Lovey tipping drinks while they relaxed on those twin bamboo loungers outside their hut.

The only time I was injured in the series was during a jungle scene. I was standing on a green apple box that was elevated for some reason I don't remember. When I stepped off it, something slippery was under me and I lost my balance and fell. When I went down, I wrenched my right knee. I could barely walk.

I was taken to the small medic station on the lot and then had to go to an orthopedic doctor in Sherman Oaks, where I was X-rayed. The doctor injected cortisone by jamming a long hypodermic needle into the inside of my knee, and I almost passed out when it penetrated. I had had all kinds of shots in the army and they didn't bother me, but this one knocked me nearly senseless.

The doctor gave me crutches and wanted me to return in a few days for the second of several shots. I told him, "You'll never see me again," handed back the crutches, hobbled out of his office, and was driven back to the studio. I went back to work that day, but not before a studio medic had me sign a waiver. My knee healed on its own, and I'm glad to report that that was the only island injury I suffered.

SEX AND THE ISLAND GIRLS

~~~~~~

S HERWOOD SCHWARTZ was the policeman on our set. This was by choice, not appointment, because he genuinely and unceasingly cared for his show. It was his baby, and he wanted to keep conflicts to a minimum and a happy cast. With any ensemble, there are bound to be differences, and Sherwood foresaw this. So he provided us an open-door policy, for which we actors were grateful because many producers have vault keepers for secretaries. No appointment, no entry. Some producers don't even want to deal slightly with the actors they have hired.

On our set, if any problems arose either with the script or with a person, we were invited to discuss it with Sherwood and attempt to resolve the matter peacefully—hopefully to everyone's satisfaction. There were times when Sherwood had to be called away from his office to come down on the set and settle something. It was evident to everyone that Sherwood tried to be fair with all of us, no matter what the request was.

When "handling" one of us—say Alan, Bob, or me—Sherwood said that any differences of opinion "always had to be settled on intellectual and logical terms." Tina, on the other hand, "spoke in non sequiturs," Sherwood says, adding that he was often dumb-founded by their conversations.

"One time, Tina refused to do a scene, for what reason I don't know," Sherwood recalls. "I had to step in to keep things going. So I went to her dressing room, where she had secluded herself, and I asked her what the problem was.

"She told me, 'This is a ridiculous scene, and I don't want to do it.' I pointed out that it was an integral scene and she would have to do it.

"Without a beat, she said to me, 'Would you have my dressing room painted gray?' "

Sherwood replayed some wonderful memories of his own sur-vival on the island in his 1988 book, *Inside Gilligan's Island: From Creation to Syndication*, which was originally titled *Having It All: How One Tiny Island Brought Me Fame, Fortune, and Migraines*.

One of his funnier stories had to do with the problem of cleavage: "Tina played most of her scenes in her light-beige V-neck gown, and somehow, between rehearsals and the time the camera rolled for actual takes, the V was mysteriously slipping down to reveal more cleavage. From time to time, I would get a phone call from the director of that episode asking me to come to the stage and make a decision. This was among my pleasanter duties as the executive producer: to gaze at Tina's bosom and decide whether or not there was too much cleavage."

Sherwood remembers being called to the set again on another day for the same problem: "I said to her, 'Tina, we'll have to do that scene over. You better stop yanking down the front of that dress.' Tina denied any such action. So I told her, 'Okay, then leave it that way. When you see this scene on the air, you'll find out you're a voice-over. The camera will be on the other people, and we'll just hear Ginger's voice.' "

Tina blurted out: "I don't know what's wrong. I'm not showing anything that everybody hasn't seen a million times before. On every TV show."

"Nevertheless," says Sherwood, "she hiked the shoulders of her dress up a few inches so that some of the cleavage disappeared."

Tina had a funny sense of humor. Sometimes she loved to be

Professor to Ginger: "Kissing on the mouth is far from sanitary, and it can lead to all sorts of bacterial transfer." (AUTHOR'S COLLECTION)

shocking, yet she'd retain that feminine side that made the character of Ginger so seductive.

There was a scene inside a hut in which Tina put on a show for the Howells, singing a breathy, sexy rendition of the French song "Alouette." She stood behind a bamboo microphone with a round rock attached to the top. For several takes, Tina closed her eyes softly, put her lips right next to it, sang to it, and stroked it. It was pretty damned suggestive, and, finally, the director had to yell, "Cut! Now, c'mon, Tina, we can't use that and you know it!"

There was something else Tina did that was funny. She used to love to shock Natalie Schafer in the morning when they were having their hair done by our hairdresser, Lillian. Tina would sit down in the chair, with Natalie and Dawn on either side of her. Tina would start in on some outrageous story about her steamy escapades from the night before just to irritate and tease Natalie, who became annoyed as hell. Natalie would protest: "Oh, please, Tina!"

Before the age of sexual-harassment suits, there was a guy on our crew who was kind of after Dawn in a playful, harmless sort of way. He was an old-timer in the business. At one time he was Bette Davis's lover when they both worked at Warner Brothers. He was a very charming man, and he drank a bit, which made him amusing at times. He told me that every time he got fired at Warner's because of his drinking, Bette Davis pulled strings and got him back on the payroll. He was one of those bawdy guys who was tougher than hell, but if you were a straight shooter with him, he could be a gentle soul. The women on our set adored him.

This guy would be working above the set, many times just watching the beauty below. It was hard not to admire Dawn's and Tina's beauty, even when you were working with them all day.

He called me over one day and said, "Will you give Dawn a message for me?"

I said, "Sure."

"Tell Dawn I'll give her five thousand dollars to have her join me in the hut and tickle my fancy—if she'll take a check!"

I delivered the message, and Dawn let out a yell and laughed. From then on, she'd embarrass him every once in a while by asking, "So where's the check?"

Sherwood also had to police the set when Dawn wore her real short shorts. Because of the censor's "intermittent navel" rule, says Sherwood, Dawn's belly button had to be hidden most of the time by her hip-huggers. Dawn couldn't believe it, but what could she do? When she could, she got away with it. She did it because she knew it wasn't a national crisis if the world noticed her navel every once in a while.

*Censors watched
Dawn's navel very
closely in the sixties.*
(PERSONALITY PHOTOS,
INC.)

Sherwood said he returned home one night after work, just exhausted from traffic duty on the set. His wife, Mildred, asked him how his day had gone and he told her, "It was rough, dear. Between Tina's breasts and Dawn's belly button, I didn't have a moment's peace."

DREAM HUT

Because sleeping and dreaming were the sole nocturnal activities on "Gilligan's Island," the writers loved to conjure up dream sequences as much as we enjoyed acting out the ridiculous hallucinations. And who says you don't dream in color? We did, beginning in our second season. In fact, we couldn't wait for the second season when we heard that we'd be filming in color. Our show was perfect for color television, with those pink island sunsets and the tropical setting. The dream sequences were pertinent: They widened the scope for more insanity.

Every one of us enjoyed doing accents, putting on wild costumes, getting made up, and stretching our imaginations. On any given day on our set you might find Alan Hale in drag or see a balding Tina Louise or Bob Denver in ashen makeup and a black

As a knave in the Cinderella dream sequence. (PERSONALITY PHOTOS, INC.)

In the Jekyll and Hyde dream sequence, Dawn played an Eliza Doolittle character. (AUTHOR'S COLLECTION)

Bobby loved playing Dracula in this dream sequence. (COURTESY OF SHERWOOD SCHWARTZ)

Skipper, shown here with Patrick Denver, was a scary giant in a "Jack and the Beanstalk" dream sequence. (COURTESY OF SHERWOOD SCHWARTZ)

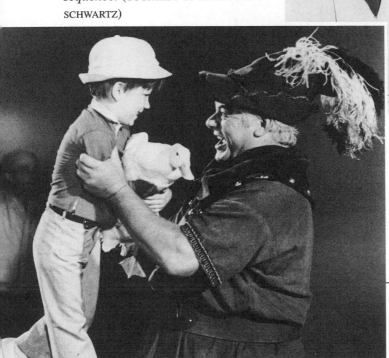

cape as Dracula. These fantasies eventually became the favorite episodes for most of us.

Jim Backus said his favorite was the one in which he played an old, crotchety prospector who has struck gold in the mountains. The Western set we used to film that episode was the dusty Dodge City street from "Gunsmoke." Jim ad-libbed a lot in those scenes and injected quite a bit of Mr. Magoo into that old prospector; I suspect that was why it was his favorite.

Natalie Schafer was quick to say her favorite episode involved Lovey's dream of the Cinderella story in which she played the tortured, ugly stepsister who magically gets an invitation to the ball via her clumsy fairy godfather (Gilligan).

Dawn Wells says she really enjoyed the Eliza Doolittle char-

The Howells were evil spies in one of Gilligan's dreams.
(COURTESY OF SHERWOOD SCHWARTZ)

The knave and the nerd in the Cinderella dream sequence.
(PERSONALITY PHOTOS, INC.)

Gilligan dreams the Castaways have aged fifty years overnight in "Meet the Meteor." (PERSONALITY PHOTOS, INC.)

acter she played in the dream in which Gilligan turned from Jekyll to Hyde at the mere mention of food ("Freeeesh Fiiiiiish!").

I'm not sure I'd pick this as my favorite, but I liked the one in which I did my Cary Grant imitation. After I filmed that, Sherwood pulled me aside and with a straight face said, "Russ, that was the best Rex Harrison I've ever seen." He still gives me trouble about that one.

There were a couple of times I had to get special makeup applied to look like a shriveled-up, hunched-over ninety-year-old man. I had a great line at the end of the "Jack and the Beanstalk" dream episode in which Gilligan rescued the goose that laid the golden oranges and saved two old prisoners from a dungeon in the giant's castle. Tina and I were made to look pretty damned filthy and ugly, since we had been trapped in there for decades by the ominous giant.

As a reward, Gilligan was kissed by the old hag, who suddenly became a beautiful princess wearing a sparkling tiara. I convinced sweet little Mary Ann that she had to kiss me so that I could be transformed, too. She hated the idea of it, but she gave in and I grabbed her in my arms like a lecher and dipped her while I kissed her. Only I didn't turn into a prince.

Disgusted, she said, "Oh, you're not a prince."

*"Well, don't believe
everything ya hear, girlie!"*
(© 1993 CBS, INC.)

"No, I'm not, am I?" I said, cackling. "Well, don't believe everything ya hear, girlie!"

That "Beanstalk" episode stuck in Alan Hale's mind because more than one fan told him that he was downright frightening as the evil giant.

Considering the way the segment was shot, it's understandable. To make Alan appear more hulking, the castle set was made miniature. The giant was mostly shot from the floor, so he towered above the camera. It was like a child's-eye view. To make the scene even more terrifying, Alan's voice was amplified and echoed and the music was eerie. The climax came when the giant finally captured Gilligan (played by Bob Denver's four-year-old son, Patrick) and lifted him up in the air as the illusion dissolved. Maybe seeing Skipper in what was more like a nightmare was a bit threatening for some kids. I'm not sure.

All I *am* sure of is that those dream sequences have always been popular with the fans. They were creamy and colorful and sometimes had lavish sets. The dreams allowed those of us stuck on the island, and you the viewer, to step off the island and into a Twilight Zone for a few minutes.

ISLAND BEASTS

I T seemed that in every other episode we had some crazed little monkey on the set, moving around, crapping on the soundstage, or getting into mischief. I recall clearly one organ-grinder monkey that was a strange-looking cuss. He was a senior citizen monkey with no teeth, but he wanted to bite me—continually. If I was sitting in my chair, he'd sidle up and start to gnaw at my arm and my hands—only he was gumming me. He found me pretty tasty one day and I pushed him away, but he kept jumping back at me. He drove me crazy.

Vito Scotti, a wonderfully versatile character actor who visited our island several times, worked closely with that dysfunctional monkey. As Boris Balinkov, an insane scientist, he put a spell on the Castaways and ruled them by walkie-talkie. Vito vividly recalls getting his fingers and his arms gnawed at, too, only the poor old monkey was even more annoying to him.

"The little monkey had to sit on my shoulder," Vito says, "and you know, monkeys are always picking. He kept picking at my hair, and I certainly didn't have fleas. I don't know what he was picking at. Just picking, picking. Then, right in the middle of the scene, he reached out and grabbed a third of my mustache—my *real* mustache—and plucked it out! He ripped a whole chunk of hair out of my face. The blood that came out of my upper lip, my God.

Vito Scotti, the man who visited the island more than any other actor, played mad scientist Boris Balinkov. Here he is in "The Friendly Physician."
(COURTESY OF VITO SCOTTI)

"I hurled that monkey up way over the scenery. He flew maybe ten feet in the air above us. Then the trainer was yelling at me, 'You could've killed my monkey!' So I said to the trainer, 'I'm gonna kill you *and* the monkey!' and I started chasing him!"

Vito also worked with a nervous, twitching parrot that left droppings on his shoulder every time there was a sudden noise or movement. This time, Vito was again dressed as the scientist, only he took the Castaways to another island, which was the only time in all of the episodes that the Castaways left their own sandy turf.

Vito recalls, "I was wearing this nice black mantle, and every time that parrot crapped on my mantle, the wardrobe person would come over and clean it up, again and again. Then with his beak, the parrot would go for my ear all the time. It was very distracting."

And with the birds, we had cats. Big cats. There was a morning at the studio that I can still see clearly. I was sitting at Keester Sweeney's makeup table, which was set up behind the cyc—our backdrop with a sky painted on it, surrounding our set. Keester was putting makeup on my face, and I was sitting facing the mirror when I looked up and saw a sleek Bengal tiger walking toward us.

All I could think to do was calmly say, "Keester, don't move a muscle. Don't turn around. There's a live tiger about forty feet away heading right toward us. Don't act like you even see it."

"There's no trainer?"

"Just a tiger." I clenched the armrests and stopped breathing for a moment while the tiger wandered around and I tried not to make eye contact with it through the mirror. His trainers started calling him from the other side of the stage, "Harry . . . here, Harry!" It seemed like an eternity until they found Harry and gently leashed him up.

I've never felt a frozen fright like that. We had a lion on another show and I wasn't apprehensive because it almost looked as if it wanted to be petted. To me, a lion is a lion, but a tiger is a tiger.

In that episode Gilligan made friends with a full-grown lion. I remember a scene in which the lion wandered out of the Howells' hut and Mrs. Howell ran away from it into the jungle. Natalie Schafer was adept at pulling off any type of crazy scheme the scripts called for and enjoyed doing so. This was something she never got working on the stage.

But, lion trainer or no lion trainer, Natalie made sure she was not going to be around that animal. She was petrified of the notion. In the read-through, Natalie had no qualms about informing Sherwood point-blank that a stand-in would be necessary for her scene because she refused to go near the beast.

That same lion gave Bob Denver a scare he has never forgotten. He was filming a scene in which Gilligan runs into the Howells' hut to escape from the lion. After he barricades their extravagant orange-chiffon-laced doors, he turns around and discovers the lion sitting on Mr. Howell's bed.

"It was six-thirty in the evening," Bob says, "and this lion was pretty tired.

"He pushed off these twin beds and leaped toward me, but the

Bob tried to make friends with the lion, but later in the day the animal lunged at him in a rage. (PERSONALITY PHOTOS, INC.)

beds split apart. He lost his momentum, and then the trainer was in midair and tackled him off the bed. He would've gotten me, except for the twin that moved. When a lion roars and it's coming at you, the hair stands up on the back of your neck. I always thought that was just a phrase that you read. You know, the writer's prerogative. Until it actually happens. That was the closest I ever came to getting hurt working on the set."

ISLE BE DAMNED

~~~~~~

Vox populi.

It means "the people's voice." That Latin phrase became most important in the survival for us Castaways on television.

It's been proven over the years that our show is a bit of an anomaly: The people's voice said they loved us Castaways, while the critics almost unanimously wanted to sink our island. They detested us. We have been considered the dregs of television, and it has never set well with any of us. As a cast, we were devastated at what critics wrote and said about us. We couldn't figure it out because we had high ratings, reached the Top Ten, and some weeks reached number three.

With their consistently bad press, the critics were raising a whipping boy named Gilligan. Our show became the prime example of bad television. I remember one critic said we were a "bad accident"; another recently called us "gourmet junk food." We're moving up.

A few weeks after we premiered in the fall of 1964, some 350 TV critics and columnists voted in a national poll and named our show "the worst new show of the season." Not since "The Beverly Hillbillies" was introduced two years earlier did the critics pounce on a show and devour it so recklessly. It became fashionable to knock us. Jim Backus used to say they weren't reviews, "they were character assassinations!"

Sherwood Schwartz saved some of these damned things, and I'm really not sure why. He explains that it might be some "deep-rooted masochistic tendency" that he carries or "the same perversity that's present in all people who work in the arts and put their efforts on public display." So, courtesy of his pasted clippings, let me give you a taste of the venom:

> "It is impossible that a more inept, moronic or humorless show has ever appeared on the home tube."
>
> RICK DUBROW, UPI

> " 'Gilligan's Island' is a television series that should have never reached the air . . . [It] is the kind of thing one might expect to find running for three nights at some neighborhood group playhouse, but hardly on a coast-to-coast TV network."
>
> HAL HUMPHREY,
> syndicated columnist

> "Without a doubt, 'Gilligan's Island' is the stinkeroo of all time . . . I have a feeling the cannibals will get them soon."
>
> FRED STORM,
> San Francisco *News Call Bulletin*

> "It's difficult for me to believe that "Gilligan's Island' was written, directed and filmed by adults . . . It marks a new low in the networks' estimate of public intelligence."
>
> TERENCE O'FLAHERTY,
> San Francisco *Chronicle*

" 'Gilligan's Island' can well go down in television history as being the series to most completely waste the talents of one of the biggest casts ever assembled for a half-hour comedy show."

ARLENE GARBER,
Hollywood *Citizen News*

"The nonsense that transpires on 'Gilligan's Island' may stir up some laughter if you're a child, or unsober, or slightly weak in the head."

DONALD FREEMAN,
San Diego *Union*

That was the kind of stuff we constantly had either to avoid or endure while we were doing the show. Sherwood tried to keep our moods up because he knows that actors can be very sensitive. He even went to the extent of calling us into a meeting one day to give us his personal guarantee that the show would grab some nice ratings. "Just wait and see," he assured us.

He was angry about the lack of understanding of what the show was attempting. We weren't curing cancer here. And it wasn't *Hamlet*. Alan Hale used to tell reporters, "What motion pictures and TV are trying to do is the same thing that radio did . . . use the person's imagination. And now it's overlooked." In other words, a little nonsense in everybody's life is not so bad.

Maybe what's worst of all is that the jabs continue to persist although the show has a following like almost no other. Johnny Carson took a swing at us at least twice a year in his monologues (*for twenty-eight years!*). I'm sure the critics who panned us from the beginning would have preferred to witness our show's burial at sea, but instead we have become flotsam along the airwaves all these years, while hundreds of situation comedies have since vanished.

But you see, our show merely filled the spot it was supposed to. We didn't pretend to be sophisticated. It *was* silly. It *was* kind of dumb. But it *was* funny. In fact, "Gilligan's Island" remains an example of well-constructed humor, and many times and in many ways it has been recognized as such.

FINALLY . . . A LITTLE PRAISE

Syndicated columnist Tom Shales recently provided some positive commentary about our show. After all the years of being accustomed to critical disdain, I nearly dropped my test tubes when I read this:

Twenty years from now, kids will probably still be laughing at "Gilligan's Island" long after the topical, provocative sitcoms—which critics are always championing—have been forgotten.

[It] was never smutty or cynical or pretentious. Nobody on "Gilligan's Island" ever needed a condom or went through menopause or puberty. Nobody made politically correct pronouncements on issues of the day. No wonder that island seems such a refuge now.

It's not that sitcoms and other entertainment shows should be dopey and frivolous, but in recent years escapism has become a devalued commodity in the TV marketplace. There's something to be said for a show on which nothing of serious social import ever happens. In fact, there's serious social import in that.

After all the abuse heaped on the series, it's time somebody dared to say that Denver and Hale did an awfully adroit job of following in slapstick footsteps left by Laurel and Hardy . . . Hale's slow burns and exasperated looks into the lens were obvious and loving homage to the immortal Oliver Hardy. Denver made a droll fool.

SOJOURNERS

~~~~~~~~~~~~~~~~~~~~~~~~~~~~~~~~~~~~~~~

I F it weren't for the twenty-some passersby who stopped at the island, the show might have passed for "believable." We had an interesting blend of celebrities visit the island, like Phil Silvers, Zsa Zsa Gabor, Strother Martin, and Don Rickles.

Outside of some native girls and a Ginger look-alike, the only woman to stumble upon us was Erika Tiffany Smith, played by Zsa Zsa Gabor. That was on an episode in which the Professor was tapped for the spotlight.

For me, that was a big show because Zsa Zsa's character was a wealthy social butterfly who had her eye on the Professor. I had to try to learn romance from Ginger in a very short period of time. I remember the episode well because it was the first of several times the script called for me to kiss Tina.

When I found out who was going to be the guest star that week, I was apprehensive about working with one of the Gabor sisters. I'll say one thing for Princess Zsa Zsa, she worked well with us. She was very professional. During the days she rehearsed and filmed the episode, the World Series was being televised. We had a portable TV stashed off to the side in the dark, and every time one of us was out of a shot, he would run to the TV and watch the ball game with the sound turned down. Zsa Zsa pitched a fit because she couldn't understand what the big deal was. She couldn't figure out why anybody would want to follow the sport in the first place.

She'd say, "Vhy the hell do you men vant to vatch this silly game for?"

The first visitor to our show was Hans Conried, who played Wrongway Feldman, a grubby old airplane pilot who has spurned civilization. Hans was a lovely man, and he enacted Wrongway again in a subsequent episode. He and I shared the same agent, and what I remember most about him was that he was very well read, a cultured gentleman.

A show like ours—by logic anyway—would be defeating its own premise if people continually found the island. We should have had

Ginger psychoanalyzes kidnapper Norbert Wiley, played by Don Rickles.
(PERSONALITY PHOTOS, INC.)

Zsa Zsa Gabor played wealthy Erika Tiffany Smith, who put the moves on the Professor. (COURTESY OF SHERWOOD SCHWARTZ)

no visitors, but, instead, the Castaways were host to a privileged handful of talented character actors who visited the island. Some of them have gone on to wonderful things.

You may remember the episode that Kurt Russell did. He was a jungle boy whom Gilligan discovers on the island. This was when Kurt was a young fellow, in his Disney days. His father, Bing Russell, was a good friend of mine, and Bing escorted young Kurt to the set each day. Kurt has fond memories of the show, I know. And I must say, he grew up to be one hell of a good actor, just like his old man.

Phil Silvers was involved with "Gilligan's Island" from the beginning because his company was in a joint venture with Sherwood Schwartz, CBS, and United Artists in producing it. Silvers came on our show once, playing a hilarious, temperamental, blowhard Hollywood producer named Harold Hecuba.

In an effort to urge Hecuba to get them rescued, the Castaways produced their own stage version of *Hamlet* with the most memorable musical selections from the opera *Carmen*. Hecuba eventually fled the island and forgot about the Castaways, of course. But because of that episode, many kids recognize the famous "Habañera" from *Carmen* without realizing it is opera. To them, it's just a catchy tune.

Kurt Russell played a jungle boy in one of the earlier episodes. (COURTESY OF SHERWOOD SCHWARTZ)

Phil Silvers is dressed as Ophelia in the Harold Hecuba one-man production of Hamlet. (COURTESY OF TOM FORRESTER)

Phil Silvers was one of a kind. Watching him work was like watching the best of Bilko. That *Hamlet* episode remains one of the most inquired-about and most popular among the fans.

One well-known actress worked on our show but was never seen. Ida Lupino was a respected actress with many film roles to her credit by the time she directed us in a handful of episodes. I had admired her work in films in the 1940s and 1950s; in 1950 she directed the first of several films, but even in the sixties there were very few female directors in television. We all respected the long career of this strong-willed woman. She was damned good. I remember she reminisced with Alan about working with his father in a motion picture years earlier. She played the wayward wife of Alan Hale, Sr., in the 1940 film *They Drive by Night* with Humphrey Bogart and George Raft.

Vito Scotti can claim the distinction of visiting the island more than any other actor. He got his unusual parts because by experimenting with wild makeup and costumes he could transform himself. In fact, most people rarely put it together that the same guy who

PRO ISLANDERS

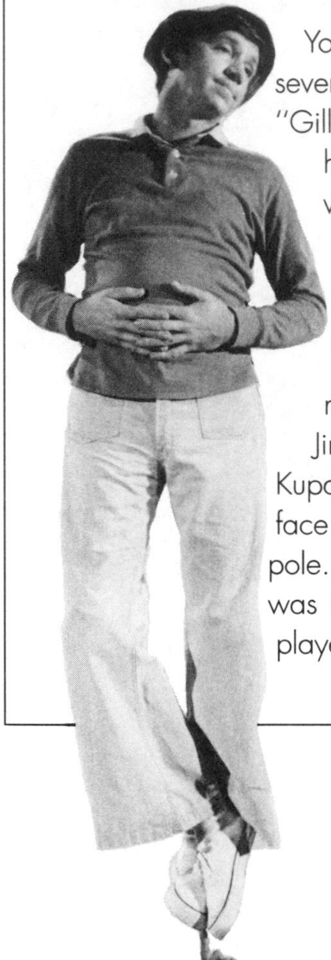

You probably didn't notice, but we had several well-known pro athletes appear on "Gilligan's Island." These guys were mostly hidden underneath native headdresses, wore only grass skirts, and were forced to yell jibberish like "Ungowa" most of the time. I think Sherwood Schwartz was very careful not to stereotype blacks in the roles of spear-chucking natives, so he put jocks in there.

Jim Lefebvre, for instance, was one of our Kupaki headhunters who mistook Gilligan's face for the face on top of a sacred totem pole. As a Los Angeles Dodger, Lefebvre was the 1965 Rookie of the Year, and he played eight seasons as an infielder for the ball club. Another Dodger ballplayer,

Basketball star
Walt Hazzard was
an air force lieutenant
in one episode.
(PERSONALITY PHOTOS, INC.)

outfielder Al Ferrara, was a screaming Kupaki in the same episode. Ferrara was the Dodger of the Year in 1967 and also played for the San Diego Padres and the Cincinnati Reds.

Walt Hazzard, the gangly basketball player who dribbled for UCLA under coach John Wooden, was on our show long before the Harlem Globetrotters appeared in our last television movie. And Denny Miller, who played basketball for UCLA, was on our show twice. You might remember him as the beefy blond surfer Duke Williams, who rode a tidal wave to the island. Denny was also Tongo the ape-man, an actor studying for a part in a jungle motion picture who, naturally, leaves the Castaways behind.

In another episode—the one in which Gilligan's vision has been distorted and he sees everything upside down—look closely and you'll find quarterback Roman Gabriel striped with greasepaint, portraying a native. Gabriel played with the Los Angeles Rams and later the Philadelphia Eagles.

played the Japanese soldier in two episodes was the same person who played Boris Balinkov. Vito told me his film idol was Lon Chaney, "The Man of a Thousand Faces."

When Vito became the Japanese soldier who didn't know the war had ended, he played it "high," which means as an obvious parody. Vito wore glasses that had lenses like the bottoms of Coke bottles, and he could barely see out of them. His depiction was hilariously stereotypical. The rule was, If you make Jim Backus laugh, you are funny. And Vito had us all laughing out loud.

Recently, Vito says, there was a story on "The CBS Evening News" about the anniversary of the bombing of Pearl Harbor. The story also stated that Japanese actors in the union are very sensitive about anyone other than a Japanese person playing their nationality.

"Right then, when Dan Rather was talking about it, they showed a clip of me from 'Gilligan's Island' as the Japanese soldier," Vito says. Back then, Vito could get away with undertaking such roles. Today it's unacceptable, and justifiably so. But Vito has a few hundred other faces he can put on, so he'll be just fine.

Vito recalls a potentially dangerous moment on 'Gilligan's Island' that he can laugh at now. Playing Balinkov in a final scene, he warned the Castaways that he'd "be back." Then he was supposed to step into a small motorboat and flee the lagoon.

"I got into this motorboat, and I pulled on the rope to start the motor," Vito says. "I let the rope go, and it caught the rope that held my mantle, which was like an exquisite black cape. The cord knotted up and pulled my face right close to the motor. I lost control of the boat, and it's running wild all over the lagoon and crossing and coming back again. I was trying to holler for help because I couldn't stop the damned thing.

"The motor had been running long enough by then that it was getting hot right next to my face," Vito continues, "and finally the boat ran aground and sort of climbed into the trees and bushes. The cameramen were laughing because they thought it was a gag, and I told them, 'Hell no, that wasn't a gag! I almost got hurt!' They wanted me to do it again. Unfortunately, they didn't have the camera rolling when I did it the first time, as I'm sure it would've looked funny on film."

THE ISLAND'S END

~~~~~~~~~~~~~~~~~~~~~~~~~~~~~~~~~~~~~~

WE never got a chance to say good-bye.

When the seven of us finished filming our ninety-eighth episode at the end of the third season, the whole production company took a break, fully expecting to spend another year on the island when we returned. Sherwood Schwartz had received an official renewal notice from the network and personally called each of us to deliver the great news that we had been "picked up."

We all celebrated in our own personal way because another year of work meant another year of financial stability in a business that's almost never stable. As actors, parents, and spouses trying to make a living, we counted on that fourth season. Then things got turned upside down in what seemed like a day.

This is what happened: CBS decided to cancel its old warhorse "Gunsmoke." The network affiliates became outraged, as did many CBS bigwigs, which forced network programmers to quickly reinstate the show. That meant sacrificing a half-hour show to make room on the schedule.

Despite healthy ratings, the network bid us aloha. Sherwood was mortified when he got the call and realized he would have to again call all of us immediately to tell us we were finished. It was embarrassing and crushing for everyone, but for Sherwood I think it was a bit more humiliating. He was heartbroken, in a state of shock, and he was very apologetic on the telephone. Of course, it wasn't his fault. So we never returned to the studio as a group. We went our separate ways without a party or a kiss or a hug. The huts were quickly dismantled, the jungle was torn down, and the soundstage was swept of sand so the space could be used for some other production.

In retrospect, I guess it was appropriate that we didn't formally say farewell, although at the time none of us would have predicted that we were merely adjourning.

It was twenty-one years until we all set foot in the same room together. Even the man who put us on the island was there that evening in May of 1988, when we all appeared on the Fox Network's "The Late Show" with host Ross Shafer. The group even included Jim Backus, who was very sick at the time, and Tina Louise, who had

The Late Show: *Although the Howells hadn't arrived yet, this reunion was the only time the entire original cast reassembled in one room. Ross Shafer was the host for the Fox Network's sixty-minute tribute to our show in 1988.* (COURTESY OF ROSS SHAFER)

always fought to sever her connection with the show. This hour-long tribute to "Gilligan's Island" was our only complete reunion, and we all felt positive about it. I thought we all looked pretty good, too.

In the interim, most of us had stayed in touch. We had remained good friends and gathered on many occasions for partial reunions, promotions, two animated cartoon series, three TV movies, and even a handful of commercials. We didn't forget about "Gilligan's Island," but what was amazing to us was that the public wouldn't let it go, either.

The first film resurrection was in 1974, when ABC placed "The New Adventures of Gilligan" on its Saturday morning lineup. The animated version of our Castaway characters was produced in a joint venture between Filmation Associates and Sherwood Schwartz. Sherwood says he "settled" on the animated series because all his attempts to sell the networks a TV movie that would "rescue" the Castaways had failed. No one would touch the idea, he says, so he was resigned to the notion that an animated series might be better than nothing.

Sherwood attempted to round up all of the original cast to resuscitate our characters, but that was impossible. Dawn Wells was living in Nashville and touring in a stage production, and Tina was the only one who decided to divorce herself from "Gilligan's Island," relinquishing custody of Ginger to Sherwood Schwartz.

Even so, the cartoon Ginger had mysteriously bleached her hair white. Sherwood explains: "We had to change her appearance. We were afraid Tina might try to sue us for using her image, so we deliberately made Ginger look different."

Providing my own, unaltered voice for a character by simply reading the script into a microphone was the easiest work I had ever had in this business. Two seasons of the cartoon show were produced, and to me it was like found money. As actors, we thought the work was casual and fun. Natalie Schafer used to say she loved doing voice-over work "because you don't have to hold your stomach in." Jim Backus was an old pro at this since he had been in front of the mike many times supplying the voice for his famous bumbling Mr. Magoo.

It was rare for all of us to be in the same studio at the same time to record our voices. Bob Denver sometimes recorded his lines separately, often in another city where he was working, so that left Alan, Natalie, Jim, and me in the studio to record maybe four scripts in an afternoon. Mary Ann's voice was provided by actress Jane Webb and Ginger's by actress Jane Edwards.

After all the tapes were recorded, an engineer edited them and spliced together the dialogue. Then the track was complete. Next, the animators drew and painted the characters according to our voices and the story line, not the other way around.

In the end, I think we made the transition from live characters to cartoon caricatures effortlessly. After all, in the original series our colorful costumes, bamboo gadgets, and tropical scenery already looked cartoonlike. For that matter, *we* looked cartoonish. The Skipper and Gilligan are as instantly identifiable as, say, Laurel and Hardy. The fact that we would draw from a built-in audience on Saturday morning was what convinced Sherwood that this cartoon might have a chance.

Our animated counterparts from "The New Adventures of Gilligan" in 1974. (COURTESY OF FILMATION ASSOCIATES)

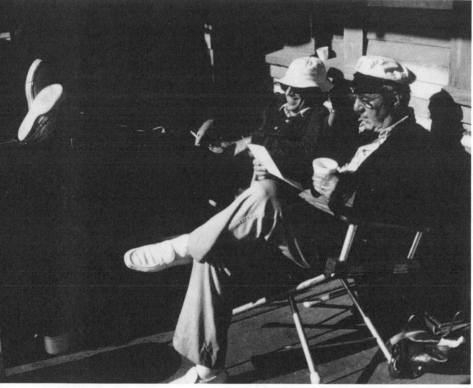

Bob enjoys a cigarette, and Jim reads some fan mail in this snapshot taken when we filmed Rescue from Gilligan's Island. (PHOTO BY SHERWOOD SCHWARTZ)

Frankly, we couldn't believe we were reviving the show because, again, none of us had much faith in the island to begin with. When we made these cartoons, we were just starting to notice that the old island was really hangin' in there for some strange reason.

THE RESCUE

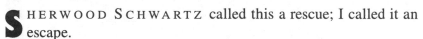

SHERWOOD SCHWARTZ called this a rescue; I called it an escape.

After fifteen years, somehow, some way, the seven stranded Castaways who needed absolutely no introduction to television audiences were finally contriving a means of reaching civilization. We were finally getting off that fictional island.

It seemed as if it would never happen. You see, ever since we had gotten canceled, Sherwood had savored the idea of someday going back and capping the open lid he had left the viewers. Ten years went by, and he couldn't sell the idea. Fifteen years approached, and finally, because fate put him in the right spot at the right time, he casually interested some NBC network executives in rescuing the Castaways. Different hands were on the network's rudders, and Sherwood's idea was seriously considered this time around.

Even though NBC was hesitant at first, Sherwood was so sure of the idea that he ended up financing the film himself. It was a gamble in many ways, the most obvious being that these waters were untested. Up until that time, there had been no such thing as "reunion movies" on television. Sherwood guaranteed only six of the seven original cast members because he knew Tina would be unobtainable.

When I got his phone call, naturally I was interested in playing the Professor again, but I wanted a little time to think about it. The original series had done some damage to my career, so I wondered if

Finally rescued after fifteen years. (AUTHOR'S COLLECTION)

this would deepen the wound. Would it be good for my career? Would it matter at all? I had a lot of thoughts about whether to do the TV movie, and one of them was that Sherwood was going to do the movie no matter who was in it. So I talked it over with my wife and we both came to the same conclusion: Yeah, do it, have a good time, and reminisce with old friends.

Tina was offered the role of Ginger in *Rescue from Gilligan's Island* and, to Sherwood's surprise, she considered it—and reconsidered it—many times. She changed her mind about five times, telling him yes, then no, then yes again. "Tina felt trapped in a role she couldn't get out of," Sherwood told us, as if we didn't know it already.

Finally, within a matter of days before the movie was to begin filming, Tina demanded what Sherwood referred to as "a Godfather sum," which was about one tenth of the movie's budget.

Tina explained her decision:

I've gone through so many emotions with the series—from resentment, to just about all of them. I felt it was not the right thing to do emotionally, or rather career-wise. Part of me wanted to do it and get back together as a reunion for old times' sake, but part of me said, "No, that's not a good idea." I felt if just one wrong person saw me [as Ginger], then it would be bad for my career. I felt, "If I do the TV movie, my price would have to be met." It actually came down to dollars and cents. It had to be worth it for me. I didn't mind asking for a large amount. Hey, Sherwood Schwartz has gone on to bigger and better houses because of "Gilligan's Island." Why not me?

Sherwood decided to recast the role and hired a tall redhead named Judith Baldwin to play Ginger. The first time the cast got together was at a meeting on the CBS lot in a conference room. We hugged and caught up with each other's lives, and we marveled at how good everybody looked. It was going to be great to work together again. The scripts were handed out, and we sat around a big conference table and had our initial read-through of the rescue.

The project started out as a two-hour movie. NBC foresaw high ratings, so the executives got greedy and decided to break it into two one-hour specials to air on succeeding Saturday nights. We filmed it on the old lagoon at CBS, which still held water, believe it or not. Some scenes that took place in the "ocean" were filmed at Paramount Studios in the huge outdoor tank, with a sky painted on a wall behind it.

Somebody suggested that the story involve Skipper and Gilligan hunting down the individuals who visited the island and terrorizing them for making the Castaways spend fifteen more hellish years there.

It was Mother Nature who had hit the island with a violent hurricane that put the rescue into motion. Because of a little metallic disc that Gilligan found, the Professor was able to activate a barometer to predict the catastrophic weather. The Castaways lashed their huts together in an effort to stay afloat. When the storm hit, the new community hut—and the patch of land beneath it—drifted out to sea.

Utilizing the Howells' vast wardrobe, the Castaways constructed a sail and Gilligan bumbled once again when he started a fire to broil some snapper. The hut caught fire and began to smoke, which attracted a Coast Guard helicopter. Their plight had ended.

Filming a scene for Rescue from Gilligan's Island *in Paramount's studio tank.* (COURTESY OF SHERWOOD SCHWARTZ)

The rescue scene was shot in Marina Del Rey, California, with sailboats and fireboats and a Coast Guard cutter surrounding the floating hut being towed into "Honolulu Harbor." It was an incredible sight. Coast Guard sirens were blasting, and people were waving. There were bands playing and hundreds, maybe thousands of extras all around the piers cheering us. Many of them were tourists who wanted to witness the rescue.

When we ambled up the gangplank to meet civilization finally, tears were streaming from many people's eyes. Including ours. At that moment, the show became a reality for us as well as the viewers. It was as if we had really been saved. In one scene we were driven through a downtown parade with confetti flying everywhere.

In the script, the Castaways finally decided to part ways and return to a faster-paced society. As the crowds scattered, the Castaways were left alone to say their good-byes. They realized how close they had become, so they vowed to keep in close touch. That scene meant a lot to us. We finally got a chance to hug and say good-bye. Officially. On film.

Meanwhile, the Professor found scientific innovations mind-boggling and Ginger realized that show business had lost its innocence. The Skipper and Gilligan tried to purchase a new charter boat, but to no avail because the Skipper was considered at fault for the original shipwreck. Mary Ann almost married her old boyfriend back home on the Kansas farm, and the Howells found out their old associates didn't think much of their island family.

The second hour of the film aired the following Saturday night. It involved a subplot about two inept Soviet spies attempting to retrieve Gilligan's good-luck charm, which happened to be a valuable plutonium disc.

A year passed, and on the anniversary of their rescue, the former Castaways got together for a cruise on Skipper's new vessel, the S.S. *Minnow II*. Once again, a storm hit while they were out on the water, and they were shipwrecked—on the same island. Again.

Emotions were running high on the last few days of production.

How nice of them to leave out my name.

(REPRINTED WITH PERMISSION FROM *TV GUIDE*® MAGAZINE. COPYRIGHT 1965, 1966 BY NEWS AMERICA PUBLICATIONS, INC.)

Re-creating a familiar pose, fifteen years after our first TV show, in Rescue from Gilligan's Island. (AUTHOR'S COLLECTION)

On the final day of filming, Alan Hale and Bob Denver clashed in a way I had never seen before.

Bob had gone out at lunchtime and tipped the ol' elbow a few too many times. We still had a couple of hours of work to do because we were going to be shooting at night on the marina. Bob came back to the set feeling pretty good. Alan was angry and told Bob off in front of all of us. Then Bob got upset and stormed off. Eventually, everyone calmed down and we got the shot that night, but it was tense for a while.

That was the only time I ever saw Bob and Alan get into it like that. As closely as they worked together for years, it was amazing that this was the only incident that I had witnessed between them. Alan and Bob always maintained a mutual respect and admiration for each other. They were very good friends.

This reunion really did make it seem as if all of us had just left for the weekend and returned on Monday to resume the series. We fell back into it quickly.

Our rescue was hyped in the press pretty heavily, but we never knew what kind of ratings tidal wave we were about to create. NBC, on the other hand, knew it had something powerful and kicked off its new season with the premiere of *Rescue from Gilligan's Island* on October 14, 1978. That night, our movie got a whopping 52 share and a Nielsen rating of 30.2. Those were phenomenal numbers. Today, *Rescue from Gilligan's Island* remains one of the highest-rated TV movies of all time.

In the years after we all parted ways in 1967, we gathered together mostly for work or a charity cause, a talk show, or a guest appearance as a Castaway on another sitcom.

The TV reunion I got charged up for was our "Family Feud" battle against the casts of "Hawaiian Eye," "Batman," and "Lost in Space." We creamed 'em.

After a week's worth of "One hundred people surveyed, top five answers on the board" from Richard Dawson, our "Gilligan's Island" team (Alan, Jim, Natalie, Dawn, and I) came out the victors, earning $23,000 for the Motion Picture and Television Fund. Even though Jim was not strong enough to stand for the taping of several shows back to back, he was given a tall bar stool, which worked perfectly. His answers always rang up the bucks, too, which just showed that he was still sharp. Dawn and I were paired for the "Fast Money" round, and we cleaned up.

Most of us have put on our old costumes, or a facsimile of it, to

Greeting the press before we competed on TV's "Family Feud."
(PERSONALITY PHOTOS, INC.)

"Good answer! Good answer!" We cleaned up on "Family Feud."
(COURTESY OF SHERWOOD SCHWARTZ)

ALF, a big fan of our show, couldn't wait to give Gilligan the snapshot horns. (AUTHOR'S COLLECTION)

appear in all types of shows and charity functions. Tina Louise surprised us when she joined most of us at a dedication ceremony of the "Gilligan's Island" waiting room at Los Angeles Children's Hospital.

You may remember that Bob and Alan sat in a box together on "Hollywood Squares" and that Natalie and Jim became Mr. and Mrs. Howell for an Orville Redenbacher popcorn ad in the early 1980s. Other shows that have paid homage to "Gilligan's Island" include "The Wild, Wild West," "ALF," "Baywatch," "The New Gidget," "New Monkees," "It's Gary Shandling's Show," "The Bob Newhart Show," and "The Simpsons." Even "Short Ribs," a Los Angeles cable variety show that starred Billy Barty and an all-dwarf cast, performed a sketch as the Castaways. In the end, they fear starvation and decide to have a little lunch—the Skipper.

Strange that the "death of a Castaway" theme has been repeated several times on TV. "SCTV," the Canadian comedy show that launched so many careers like Martin Short's and Catherine

O'Hara's, did a takeoff of "Masterpiece Theatre" with a segment called "Cretin's Island." In the sketch the Skipper (John Candy) choked Cretin (Joe Flaherty), and the Professor (Dave Thomas) provided the cause of death: "His esophagus has collapsed!"

I think the last public appearance Jim and Natalie did together was a segment of "Lifestyles of the Rich and Famous." How appropriate.

MORE TV MOVIES AND REUNIONS

W H A T Sherwood really wanted was to produce a movie called *Murder on Gilligan's Island*. I'm not sure whether he ever got the concept down on paper, but I recall his being very excited about the idea. "I just love the title," he said. It's a shame that the film never happened because even the title would have piqued more curiosity than the two movies we made instead.

Following *Rescue from Gilligan's Island*, the network knew it had a good thing. Our record-breaking success in *Rescue* prompted Sherwood to use his powers as Lazarus to keep us alive on the island for two more TV movies, *The Castaways on Gilligan's Island* and *The Harlem Globetrotters on Gilligan's Island*. In both of these adventures, we were not alone on the island. We were rescued again, and Mr. Howell built a bamboo tropical resort for tourists. The whole idea was to host celebrity guests à la *The Love Boat* and *Fantasy Island*, which were on the air at the time.

All right, all right. So these weren't the best TV movies in the world, but the ratings they received *were* respectable, and I'm positive that Sherwood was gearing up to put us on another uncharted island in weekly installments if a network would agree. Audiences kept tuning in to see what we looked like after all those years. But things were nearing the end; I could see it.

Our second TV movie: The Castaways on Gilligan's Island. (COURTESY OF
SHERWOOD SCHWARTZ)

In *Castaways*, a ninety-minute movie, we were stranded on the
same island again. Gilligan stumbled upon two disabled World War
II fighter planes and a machine shop in a Quonset hut that we had
somehow overlooked all the years we were on the island. I combined
parts from the planes and flew us off the island, only the plane
cracked up and we had to make an emergency landing back on the
island. The Coast Guard spotted us and this time we were instantly
rescued.

Mr. Howell transformed the island into a resort paradise, and—
imagine!—he allowed all of us to be partners in the venture. Of
course, Gilligan and Skipper still slept in hammocks that hung in a
hut, and the rest of us were dressed in the same clothes we had worn

I drew from my experience in the war when we filmed these scenes in an abandoned airplane for The Castaways on Gilligan's Island. (PHOTO BY SHERWOOD SCHWARTZ)

Once again attempting to get off the island in The Castaways on Gilligan's Island. (COURTESY OF SHERWOOD SCHWARTZ)

for fifteen years, prowling the new resort like costumed mascots at a theme park. The guests in this special were Tom Bosley and Marcia Wallace. The movie aired in March 1979.

The ratings were modest. None of us really expected to put on those costumes again, but Sherwood resuscitated the crew and passengers of the S.S. *Minnow* one more time.

Sherwood, along with NBC, played around with the idea of having the Dallas Cowboy cheerleaders come to the island resort. Those plans were thwarted by scheduling problems for the Texas beauties. Instead, the Harlem Globetrotters crash-landed near the island and became the guests in this 1981 TV movie, which also involved a subplot with a robot and the Howells' nemesis, J. J. Pierson. Somewhere in there, Thurston Howell IV (played by David Ruprecht) appeared out of nowhere to handle his father's business affairs while the patriarch was out of town.

The new Ginger for this TV movie—the third titian-haired actress to play the movie star—was Constance Forslund. She even reprised Ginger's nightclub routine, singing "I Wanna Be Loved by You." Also in the cast were guests Martin Landau, Barbara Bain, Scatman Crothers, and Bob Denver's wife, Dreama.

This really was the end of the end, and most of us from the original cast knew it. At some point between *Castaways* and *Globetrotters*, Alan had suffered a blood clot in his leg that caused complications throughout his body. He was ordered by his doctors to drop some weight and quit smoking. He was noticeably thinner in *Globetrotters*, and so was Jim Backus, who was so ill that he only came in at the end of the film for a quick cameo appearance, delivering a few lines and leaving. Originally, Jim's doctor advised him not to participate at all.

So Jim wasn't scheduled to be in the film, but his wife, Henny, called Sherwood and said she thought he might be able to do something brief. "It might be just the thing he needs to lift his spirits," Henny told Sherwood. In one day, Sherwood rewrote the final scene to accommodate Thurston Howell III. And it was just like old times.

When his scene was completed, Henny led Jim arm in arm to the soundstage doors. They walked very slowly. The whole crew and all of us in the cast applauded Jim because we knew this might be the last time this trouper would be joining us. I looked over at Natalie. She had just given Jim a big kiss and a hug, and tears welled in her eyes as she waved good-bye to her Thurston. Jim turned and blew us a kiss.

The Castaways on Gilligan's Island. (COURTESY OF SHERWOOD SCHWARTZ)

Sweet Lou Dunbar and Curly Neal guest-starred in our last TV special, The Harlem Globetrotters on Gilligan's Island. (COURTESY OF SHERWOOD SCHWARTZ)

Some of the cast got together in 1988 at a book-signing event in Los Angeles. (PHOTO BY STEVE COX)

Gilligan's face has been seen in almost every area of pop culture over the years. Not only does Disney World have a "Gilligan's Island" set re-created in its Disney-MGM theme park, but there have been quite a few items merchandised on the series: Topps bubble-gum cards, T-shirts and sweat-shirts, a 1960s Whitman hardback storybook, a 1970s floating bathtub play set made by Playskool, Whitman's "Gilligan's Island" coloring book, a Nintendo game, a Bally pinball machine, and Gilligan and Skipper bend-able figures. Most recently, the episodes have become available in deluxe boxed sets from Columbia House Home Video, by subscription only.

SKIPPER'S HAT

If the Smithsonian Institution could display just two items to represent "Gilligan's Island," they would be Gilligan's flimsy white hat and Skipper's black cap.

Bobby says he saved about two of the dozens of stretched-out hats he went through over the years, but Alan's original black cap, the one that went through most every episode in the series, was uniquely presented to Sherwood Schwartz by its grateful owner.

Alan spoke of the gesture a few years ago. "Having great admiration for Sherwood," he said, "I took the hat and had it bronzed, like baby shoes if you will, and I think he was very taken by it. It's in his library now, and I thank him for accepting it."

What started out as an ornamental piece of Alan's costume and a prop to pop Gilligan became a natural part of his daily appearance—long after the series ended. Every few years or so, Alan would make a trip down to a marine supply store in Long Beach and load up on a supply of Skipper caps. And he never seemed to go anywhere without one atop his dome. He wore it to the store, he played golf with it on, and, whenever one of the caps had seen one too many days, Alan gave it to a fan. It got to be such a part of him that Alan looked odd without it.

The caps he wore later on were not always black. Some were white with ornate gold trim, and on a few of them there was a small, green gemstone in the center of the gold-anchor insignia embroidered on the front. Whenever Alan played in celebrity golf tournaments around the country, he proudly placed his cap in the charity auction. Top price fetched for an authentic Skipper's cap: $750.

"That's how aware people are of 'Gilligan's Island' and the Skipper," Alan said.

And for you trivia mavens, Alan's hat size was $7^3/8$.

(COURTESY OF SHERWOOD SCHWARTZ)

REEF MADNESS

~~~~~~

IF ever a group of actors was typecast, it was us. Every single one of us. It was like the Curse of Kona. We all felt the struggle to get roles after our three years on the island. We all knew it about each other, although we never sat around and dwelt on the fact or drowned our sorrows together around Jim Backus's bar.

From the time I started making a living in 1950 until "Gilligan's" in 1964, I had basically played heavies—you know, the bad guy. I had some straight roles, but mostly I was known as a "character heavy" to the casting people.

Then "Gilligan's" came along, and after the show was over, I couldn't get a job playing heavies. Producers would say, "What are you talking about? Are you kidding?"

The turnover in Hollywood is amazing, and, especially today, many people have only been exposed to me as the kind, sensible, reasonable Professor. It took quite a while before people would accept me as anything but that type. It was a very difficult period in my life and in my career.

In those days, as a television actor you rarely slid from one series into the next. You were in limbo for a while. It happened to you, but you didn't want it to. A lot of actors secretly hoped a new series would miraculously beam around them.

The whole system of auditions is different today. Before "Gilligan's," I got work because of my previous work or because I had worked with the director or the producer on an earlier picture. Today, they call you in to read for the part if you've got just three lines. Think of it: here you've been in the business for forty years and some jerk calls you in for a three-line bit and says, "Hey, I wanna see what you can do." It's maddening.

I was auditioning for a feature film after "Gilligan's" and some twenty-four-year-old casting associate said, "Tell me a little about your career."

Frustration stole my patience. All I could blurt out was, "Where the hell have *you* been? I'm sorry," I told the kid, "I've been working here for twenty-five years ... don't you know anything about me?"

He gave an excuse that he was from the East Coast. I said, "Your job as a casting person is to have some idea as to who you're talking to. I'm not new, *you* are."

Natalie Schafer told me that had happened to her, but she had a remedy: If a casting director sat back and said to her, "Tell me a little about yourself," she'd say, "You first."

"Gilligan's Island" hasn't left the television airwaves since it began. Immediately following our cancellation from prime time in 1967, we were stripped into daytime television in many markets around the country and abroad. This is called syndication, which means the reruns are rerun and rerun again and again, in different cities, and on national cable networks. So, when we say that "Gilligan's Island" has never left television, it's the truth.

Sherwood Schwartz says "Gilligan's Island" has been repeated more often in more places than any other television show in history. Fans assume that we all became as rich as Howells from this show. But it boils down to this: Two years after the show, each of us was paid in full, and from then on we've made nothing. Zip. Zero. Zilch.

When the show was canceled, the cast was offered either the usual decreasing residuals or an immediate buy-out of our contracts, which added up to fifty cents on the dollar, which we promptly rejected.

The executives knew what they were doing when they negotiated with us. I remember they completely deflated the whole show in front of us: "We've only got three seasons . . . The black and whites aren't appealing . . . This show will be quickly forgotten." The show's owners (Gladasya Productions, CBS, and United Artists) were trying to screw us, and none of us wanted to take their offer.

One thing you realize in this business: Nobody gives you anything. You get paid a certain sum because in the end someone else is making triple, five, or ten times that.

If I only had a dollar for every time the show has aired somewhere.

STUCK ON GILLIGAN'S ISLAND

~~~~~~~~~~~~~~~~~~~~~~~~~~~~~~

W E' V E always had the greatest fans. Ask any one of us Castaways. Fans have always felt free about coming up to us any time, anywhere, but always with a smile. We've even attracted sophisticated fans like Walter Cronkite, who was a good friend of Alan Hale's. Gregory Peck once told Jim Backus that he never missed "Gilligan's Island." Bette Davis used to love having lunch with us on the set.

Our show's appeal knows no parameters, it seems. Bob Denver told me one time there was a Hawaiian family—two parents and a few children—who stood outside his home when he had a little place on the island of Kauai. The family sang the theme song at 6:00 A.M. until Bob finally poked his head out the window.

Bob really does enjoy sailing, so he dreads it when he's got to rent a boat. Believe me, he's heard 'em all, and it's always the same: "Three-hour tour, huh? We'll never see this boat again, will we?"

As an actor on television, if you get the chance to see the public and meet with your show's fans, the unmistakable power of the medium becomes apparent. You feel the vibrations of things you did a trillion years ago. We have all felt the impact of our television series, and we have all been aware that children make up the largest percentage of our viewers.

Kids really clung to Alan, as they cling to the Santa Claus myth. Sherwood Schwartz remembers a time when he and Alan visited a room in a children's hospital where a little boy had just had a kidney removed. The boy was beginning to stir from the anesthesia, and Alan was standing at the foot of his bed when he came out of it. Sherwood recalls:

> When his vision started to clear, he looked at Alan in disbelief. His eyes suddenly opened wide, and his face filled with wonder. In a voice that wasn't much more than a whisper, he said "Skipper?" . . . Alan, as usual, knew exactly the right thing to say. "That's right, son. The Skipper is here with you. Everything's going to be fine now." A smile appeared on the boy's face, and he closed his eyes and fell asleep.

That's one of the satisfying aspects of being a celebrity. Unanimously, we, the cast of "Gilligan's," have found it astonishing that the program we finished thirty years ago still has an impact on children. And those children have carried their affection for the show well into parenthood and trust "Gilligan's Island" with their own children as if we were family. And so, the cycle builds momentum. But adult fans can sometimes be more awkward and embarrassing than their children.

My first wife, Kay, and I were in awe when we visited Westminster Abbey in 1979. This ancient edifice, located in the very heart of London, is the burial place for some of the greatest figures in Western history—from royalty like Queen Elizabeth I to great thinkers like Sir Isaac Newton and leaders like Winston Churchill. While we were in the cathedral, a group of people, maybe twenty of them, surrounded my wife and me. Here we were, in the center of this legendary house of worship, and people were pushing pens and paper in front of my face, asking if they could have my autograph. Every one of them had cameras, and some of them were shooting home movies of me. I was embarrassed, and I was annoyed, because I did not want to do this kind of thing in what I considered a hallowed place.

I kept asking the people, "Please, please, not in Westminster

The three smokers on the island rehearsing a scene. Notice Alan's cigarette and the coconut ashtray. (AUTHOR'S COLLECTION)

Abbey. This is a church." I told them I would be happy to do all of that outside, and I *still* had to plead with them to let my wife and I enjoy the abbey in privacy. And I have to add that these were American tourists, not Brits. These things happen.

Really, though, fans are fun. When I was doing a guest spot on a sitcom a few years ago, one of the episode's writers—a young guy in his early twenties—came up to me and asked if I'd sign an autograph, but he asked for something specific. He wanted me to write "Thanks for saving my life in 'Nam." And that made me laugh. So I wrote it.

At a science-fiction convention in Baltimore, I made a personal appearance to discuss some of the films I made in the fifties, and I was amazed when nearly 90 percent of the questions that fans asked were about "Gilligan's Island." When I sat to autograph photos and such, a stream of fans had gone to a nearby grocery store and emptied the grocer's stock of coconuts. These fans rubbed smooth an area of the coconut and had me sign it with one of those silver paint pens. I couldn't believe it!

I remember a few years back when I was buying some tools and supplies in Builders Emporium, a huge hardware outlet store in Los Angeles. I took my items up to the counter and this twenty-five-year-old checker just looked at me with a straight face and said, "Are you going to fix the radio?"

My wife, Connie, reminded me of the time she and I were living in Malibu, California, near the beach. We were driving up the Pacific Coast Highway heading home, and we were hungry, so we decided to stop and get some Chinese takeout at this little hole-in-the-wall place we had heard was good. There was a Chinese guy behind the counter and another customer waiting around. The Chinese guy looked up at me and said, "Ah, you the Professor from 'Gilligan's Island'!"

I said, "Yes, I am."

"Boy, you old."

There are a lot of weird fan stories, but one of the stranger incidents happened to Alan Hale. Alan and his wife, Trinket, were eating in a small seafood restaurant one night. Alan was sporting his Skipper's hat when he walked in, and he was instantly recognized; the Hales were not looking for the celebrity treatment, but they got it anyway from the waitress and patrons. As usual, Alan was happy to sign autographs, but he preferred doing it after his meal, while he was having his coffee. So he requested his star-struck waitress kindly to head off anyone approaching until they had finished eating; then, fans would be welcome to visit his table.

After a stream of eager fans had met the Skipper, the waitress handed Alan his check and shyly asked for just one more autograph, this time for herself. She said, "Captain Kangaroo, you were one of my favorites." Alan was polite and signed something on the restaurant check. Then she left clutching her paper that Alan had signed, "All the best, Capt. Kangaroo."

I remember another of Alan's favorite anecdotes. Sometime in the years between the series and the "Gilligan's" TV movies, Alan and

Trinket flew to Yugoslavia for his appearance in the film *Curse of a Faithful Wife*. This was during some turbulent political weather in that area, so they were taking a bit of a risk.

When the Hales landed at a refueling point in Beirut, Trinket and Alan decided to deplane and walk around the airport for a while. Trinket led the way out of the plane. A sixteen-year-old soldier wearing a bandanna around his head was holding a machine gun at the bottom of the steps. He was motioning to her with his gun to remain on the plane. Alan was alarmed and moved in front of Trinket to see what was going on. The young soldier suddenly smiled and started yelling out, "Skipper! Skipper!" Can you believe it? Halfway around the world, and he still couldn't escape the recognition. Alan loved it that way, though.

Natalie Schafer loved to use the Howell name to her advantage. "My telephone lines were down from a storm, so I called the telephone company and got nowhere," she said. "Then I told them I played Mrs. Howell on 'Gilligan's Island,' and they sent a man right over!"

Dawn Wells has had some wonderful fans approach her. And she's also had a few scary moments and frightening pieces of correspondence. A lot of actors get mail from crazies, and Dawn has received some doozies that have really shaken her up. For an actor or actress, the fear of being stalked is not always paranoia. There have been a

Alan didn't seem to age over the years. This photo was taken in 1988. (PHOTO BY STEVE COX)

few fans with a fascination for our show or with one of the cast members whom I would label unhealthy. It happens, believe me, but those cases are few.

Dawn has always loved her fans, and I think she was the cast member who received the most fan mail when we were doing the show. She once boarded a commercial airline and the whole plane burst into the "Gilligan's" theme song, if that tells you anything. Dawn told me about a trip she took to Germany in which two fans at one of King Ludwig's castles in Bavaria came running up to her saying, "Mary Ann! Mary Ann!"

Outside of our "reunion" television specials and a few sitcoms like "ALF," on which we once again became Castaways for the camera, some of us have participated in promotions and tie-ins for the show. Natalie Schafer and Jim Backus even appeared as the Howells with Orville Redenbacher in one of his popcorn commercials in the mid-1980s. A couple of years ago, Bob Denver promoted a "Gilligan's" 1-900 telephone trivia line that awarded prizes.

At our personal appearance in Chicago, fan Scott Michaels presented Dawn with a Honeybee pin (as a symbol of the episode in which the girls formed a rock group called the Honeybees). (COURTESY OF SCOTT MICHAELS)

Four of us guest-starred on an episode of "ALF" on NBC. (COURTESY OF SHERWOOD SCHWARTZ)

Usually any live appearances we have made have taken place with a tropical motif, luaus and boat races and such, where fans can meet us and take snapshots.

One of the more ingenious "Gilligan's" promotions was a cast get-together orchestrated as a real "Three-Hour Tour" on a luxury excursion boat that held about four hundred people, most of whom had won the cruise in radio station contests and giveaways. They frequented the open bar and drank mai tais from coconut halves while in-person DJs blasted live music.

The tour, originating from the shore of Lake Michigan in Chicago, had gone on an hour's joyride before we boarded. We Castaways waited on a pier, at a prearranged location, and at the appropriate moment, we shot off a flare gun and the excursion boat loaded with fans arrived to "rescue" us.

"The rest" in 1990. (COURTESY OF DAWN WELLS)

Coast Guard sirens were blasting as we boarded. Fans were screaming, applauding, and singing the theme song when Alan, Bob, Dawn, and I were ushered onto this cruiser full of baby boomers. Beautiful women in grass skirts placed leis around our necks and greeted us with kisses. Camera flashes were popping in our faces, and in seconds we were surrounded.

People kept saying to me that they couldn't believe they were on a tour boat with us. It was a madhouse, but we loved every second of it. We did several of these promotions, in Baltimore, Chicago, New York, and Milwaukee.

It was on Baltimore's Chesapeake Bay "Rescue Cruise" that two fans, at separate moments, edged their way through the crowd, determined to talk to me.

I was floored when they both informed me that they had graduated from Johns Hopkins University and had gone into their respective professions because of me. One of the fans was a woman in her thirties, who had received her degree in physics.

Later on that night, a guy approached me and introduced himself. He explained that when he was a child, the Professor had inspired him, and he had also graduated from Johns Hopkins, with a degree in chemistry. I couldn't have been more gratified.

SHERWOOD SCHWARTZ ON THE IMPACT OF "GILLIGAN'S ISLAND"

~~~~~~~~~~~~~~~~~~~~~~~~~~~~~~

SO M E people not only loved "Gilligan's Island," they *believed* in it, as I learned one day when I got an unusual phone call at my office.

My secretary, Edna, interrupted my work over the intercom: "Commander Doyle is on the phone, Mr. Schwartz."

"Commander Doyle?"

"Yes. United States Coast Guard," she said.

I didn't know Commander Doyle of the United States Coast Guard, and I couldn't imagine what he wanted, but I'm very impressed by people like generals and admirals and commanders, considering the fact that I spent my army career as a corporal.

I pressed the lighted button.

"Commander?"

"Mr. Schwartz? This is Commander Doyle of the United States Coast Guard . . . I understand producers are very busy people, but I wonder if I could have an appointment with you?" he asked. "I guess I could tell you about this on the phone, but I don't know whether you would believe me. I'd rather show it to you."

A few days later the commander showed up at my office . . . I told him I was intrigued by his call, and he sat down. He was in uniform, he was in his early forties, and he looked very much like an officer in the Coast Guard.

"Well, like I said on the phone, I didn't think you would believe this unless I showed you these."

"Show me what?"

"These," Commander Doyle said, and he took a batch of envelopes from his pockets and placed them on my desk. They were telegrams and I read a few. Some were addressed to Hickam Field in Honolulu, some to Vandenberg Air Force Base, and some to other military bases. While the words varied from one telegram to another, they all said substantially the same thing:

For several weeks now, we have seen American citizens stranded on some Pacific island. We spend millions in foreign aid. Why not send one U.S. destroyer to rescue those poor people before they starve to death.

These telegrams were not jokes. They were serious wires from concerned citizens—*adult* citizens!

ISLAND FEVER

S OMETIMES I've wondered if people take "Gilligan's Island" too seriously. It amazes me how even today, people assume it's hip to pose this bright revelation by asking, "Why would the Howells bring all of that money along on a three-hour tour?" Man, it doesn't take any gray matter to figure *that* out.

You don't know how many stand-up comics owe money to Gilligan's for writing their material for them. Our show has been fodder for their routines for years. They pose all kinds of riddles. "How come the Professor could build a nuclear reactor, but he couldn't build a boat to get them off the island?" (And I never built a nuclear reactor.)

Of course, our show was inconsistent and incongruous. Of course, there are unanswered questions. At first, we asked the same questions, and then we just accepted it all and stopped wondering. Jim Backus explained it perfectly for a reporter a few years ago:

"The question we always get is, 'Where did [the Castaways] get all those clothes?' I always say, 'They had a very large suitcase.' What's funny is that they never think that's a phony answer. They wink; they're in on the joke. After all these years, they are still in on the joke."

My answer: "It's in the script."

In fact, it's in the theme song. Do you realize the lyrics lie to you? Think about it: "The mate was a mighty sailing man"? C'mon now.

"If not for the courage of the fearless crew, the *Minnow* would be lost . . ." *Would be* lost? We *were* lost.

And it wasn't a desert isle. It was a jungle island.

So your imagination gets a workout—or your gullibility, depending on how you look at it. Sure Mr. Howell brought along his stock certificates for the Tahatcha-Pookoo Oil and Mining company. Sure Mr. Howell packed an Indian chief's headdress in his trunks of clothing. Once you get past the insanity of it all, it's not so bad.

One question that is often posed to me involves the Professor's total lack of sexual interest. Was he asexual? He didn't even know how to kiss a woman affectionately.

The answer is that Sherwood Schwartz did not want to get into the sexual natures of the characters too deeply, outside of the obvious, like the Howells' devotion to each other and Ginger's lusty one-liners. Keep in mind, the consensus from the cast in the beginning was that we were targeting this show toward children. The fact that adults came along was a surprise to all of us. As time went by, it became more sophisticated, if you'll allow me that. We could see how the scripts would grab some adults.

DAWN WELLS ON RUSSELL JOHNSON

I must admit, I've always found Russell very sexy. I just adore him. He is such a sweet friend. I have a real love and fondness for him that started when we met. Now don't get me wrong, there was never any hanky-panky between any of us in the cast. But it's true, wherever I go, women come up to me and say, "Wow, I really had a crush on the Professor."

We had never met before working together as the Professor and Mary Ann. From the very beginning, Russell and I were sort of thrown together as "the rest," and from that point on we became great friends. Strong friends. It's the kind of relationship in which if I ever got into any trouble, one person I could count on would be Russell. So, whenever I have sent notes and cards to him, I usually sign them, "Love, the rest."

Russell is very different from the Professor in that he's probably one of the funniest men I've ever known. He has such a quick wit. Of course, from "Gilligan's Island" you'd never know he had any real sense of humor at all because he was such a sobering, stabilizing factor among the characters. In reality, I think Russell held things together for us as a cast as well, and that was important.

On a professional level, it was noticeable that Russell loved what he did, and he was always prepared and thorough in his work. He's a good actor, and I think he taught me a lot in the process because "Gilligan's Island" was my training ground in television. I was fortunate to have Russell—as well as the other talented cast members—as my family and my tutors in television.

One of the funniest things I remember about Russell was a public appearance we did right after the show went off the air. It was a stop at Folsom Prison. Russell and Jack Palance and I went to this maximum security prison to entertain the inmates, and we

Attending a CBS affiliates' conference, where this portrait was on display. (AUTHOR'S COLLECTION)

(PHOTO BY GABI RONA)

were supposed to do some kind of skit or something. I remember the prison officials were very concerned about security because here I was as Mary Ann in these very short shorts and all. It ended up that Russell got more hoots and whistles than I did! I think it was the first time in his life that he felt endangered like that. I told him, "Now you know how it feels."

Love to you, Russell!

"The rest"

GROWING UP WITH THE PROFESSOR

MY kids grew up always having people stare at our table in restaurants. In school, it was sometimes assumed that "if you're the Professor's kid, then you *must* have an unbelievable IQ." Sound crazy? You'd be surprised what people think. And when my kids began dating, the notion of bringing someone home to meet their parents might have been a bit uncomfortable. Especially when the Professor is standing there advising them, "Don't be out too late." I don't know why, but some of my daughter's dates were petrified. I think she didn't prepare them.

All in all, maybe it wasn't so bad for David, Kim, and my stepson, Courtney. Sure, I made my mistakes as a parent, but I'm very proud that I've raised children who have taken responsibility for themselves. In today's world, that's an accomplishment.

I thought it might be fun to have them say a few words about visiting the set of "Gilligan's Island" and growing up marooned with the Professor.

This is my son, David:

"I was on the set of 'Gilligan's Island' maybe six or seven times in the course of the three years. The time I remember most was on my

My family (clockwise behind me): My stepson, Courtney Dane; my son, David; my daughter, Kim; my wife, Connie. My grandson, Max, is peeking out from under the table. (PHOTO BY MICHAEL KORHONEN)

ninth birthday, I think. My whole class—maybe twenty-five or thirty kids—all went to the set for the afternoon to watch the filming. We got a tour of the place and went out to the lagoon. And later on, we had a little party.

"What I remember most about being in the studio was how they tried to keep us all as quiet as possible during the filming, and, later, the whole class was introduced to the cast. The actors were all nice, especially Dawn Wells. She was always good with kids, I think. On that day anyway, I think I was the hero of the class."

(PHOTO BY
MICHAEL KORHONEN)

This is my daughter, Kimberly:

"I always had the illusion that my dad was the smartest man in the world. Not only because he was my dad, and when you're a kid, your dad can beat up anybody. But also because he was the Professor. I remember thinking that he should be the President, he was so smart.

"David and I both had little TVs in our bedrooms, and whenever I got punished, Mom or Dad would take the TV privileges away for a week or so and the only thing I was allowed to watch was 'Gilligan's Island.' I'd beg my dad to watch it and say, 'Please, please, please.' He naturally gave in.

"I was on the set when Dad was filming the episode with Zsa Zsa Gabor, and I thought she was trying to marry Dad. I was pretty young, and I remember hating her because I thought she was going to take him away from my mom.

"And I remember Bob Denver lifting me up and putting me in his director's chair. It was one of those tall director's chairs. He put his white cap on my head and let me wear it for a while. He was very nice, and so was Dawn Wells. She was so sweet to me. And, of course, I'm convinced Alan Hale was the kindest man that ever lived."

This is my stepson, Courtney:

"Russell and my mom were friends for many years, so I can't remember not knowing him. I remember Russell's pal was Guy

Williams from 'Lost in Space,' and it was always exciting seeing both of them.

"What's funny to me is how fans of any age become children again when they meet Russell. They tend to say the same thing: 'You remember when you made that invention out of the radio and Gilligan drank the radioactive liquid you made?' And Russell says, 'I sure do.' Then later he'd admit, 'I didn't know what the hell they were talking about.'

"Russell can be easily embarrassed by fans sometimes. I remember one time, Russell was going down to 7-11 and I asked him if he'd cash some quarters in for me. It was like twenty dollars' worth of quarters. When he got there, he pulled all the quarters out of his pocket and they sprayed all over the floor. They rolled everywhere. So there he was on the floor, groping for quarters out from under the Twinkies stand, and some lady comes up to him and says, 'Hey, didn't you used to play the Professor on 'Gilligan's Island'?' "

My kids all live in the Los Angeles area now and have their own joys and struggles that go along with life and society in general. Courtney works in the construction field and is busy raising his bright little son, Max, who is chock-full of charisma. Kim is an actress who entered the profession under her own volition, believe me. I warned her of the perils of such a career because an actor's life can be brutal and employment can be sparse. But this is what she wanted to do, and this is what she does. She's very good at it, and I can only wish her luck because she has the talent.

David was a computer programmer before he became the first AIDS coordinator for the City of Los Angeles for a few years. His primary responsibility was the administration of several million dollars for housing, and the construction of hospices, as well as the development of educational programs about AIDS. While David worked as the AIDS coordinator, his most important contribution, I feel, was the creation of the AIDS Policy for the city. He fought long and hard to get that through governmental red tape—not to mention the depressing lack of public concern, which is just now beginning to change.

David has to take it easy these days, and he has left his job because of personal health reasons. You see, my son has the very disease that he fought so diligently against during the course of his career as the AIDS coordinator. As they say, AIDS is not restricted demographically; sooner or later, everyone will come in contact with an individual who has AIDS.

I would simply like you to know about the strength and bravery of my son. He's an extraordinary fellow who doesn't deserve this illness. There isn't a person on this earth who deserves AIDS.

THE SHIP'S LOG
98 ADVENTURES ON THE ISLAND

~~~~~~~~~~~~~~~~~~~~~~~~~~~~~~~~~~~~

(Willy) Gilligan . . . . Bob Denver
Jonas Grumby ("The Skipper") . . . . Alan Hale, Jr.
Thurston Howell III. . . . . Jim Backus
Lovey Wentworth Howell . . . . Natalie Schafer
Ginger Grant . . . . Tina Louise
Professor Roy Hinkley . . . . Russell Johnson
Mary Ann Summers . . . . Dawn Wells
Radio Announcer . . . . Charles Maxwell
    (in most every episode although uncredited)

W: Written by
D: Directed by
GC: Guest Cast
(DS): Denotes episode with a dream sequence

1. TWO ON A RAFT Gilligan and Skipper build a bamboo raft and set out to sea. After a shark attacks them, they're beached on an island they think is inhabited by Marubi headhunters. Actually, they're back on the same island as the rest of the Castaways. W: Lawrence J. Cohen and Fred Freeman, D: John Rich.

2. HOME SWEET HUT   Due to an impending tropical storm, the Castaways build a community hut. All of them get on each other's nerves, so they decide to branch out and make their own individual huts. W: Bill Davenport and Charles Tannen, D: Richard Donner.

3. VOODOO SOMETHING TO ME   Skipper professes his belief in native superstitions and thinks that Gilligan has been transformed into a monkey via voodoo witchcraft. W: Austin Kalish and Elroy Schwartz (Sherwood's brother), D: John Rich.

4. GOODNIGHT SWEET SKIPPER   Somehow the Professor can't fix the radio in this one, but he can hypnotize Skipper so he'll recall how to transform the radio into a transmitter so they can contact "The Vagabond Lady," a female pilot who is flying over the island. W: Dick Conway and Roland MacLane, D: Ida Lupino.

5. WRONGWAY FELDMAN   The Castaways discover they aren't the only ones on the island. Forgotten aviator Wrongway Feldman, who had disappeared thirty-three years earlier, is living on

Inept pilot Wrongway Feldman was on the island before we got there. Actor Hans Conried was our first guest star. (JOE WALLISON COLLECTION)

the island as well. When the Professor attempts to fix Wrongway's old prop airplane, someone persists in sabotaging the aircraft. Wrongway finally makes it off the ground, but can't remember the island's coordinates for the authorities. W: Lawrence J. Cohen and Fred Freeman, D: Ida Lupino, GC: Hans Conried (Feldman).

6. PRESIDENT GILLIGAN   Nobody will dig a well for fresh water, so an election for an island president is set. One Castaway bribes the other and finally Gilligan is elected by a write-in vote. W: Roland Wolpert, D: Richard Donner.

7. THE SOUND OF QUACKING (DS)   The Castaways are running out of food when a blight cuts off their supply of nourishment. A wild duck lands on the island, and a decision has to be made whether to eat the bird or let it fly back to the mainland with a message attached to it like a carrier pigeon.

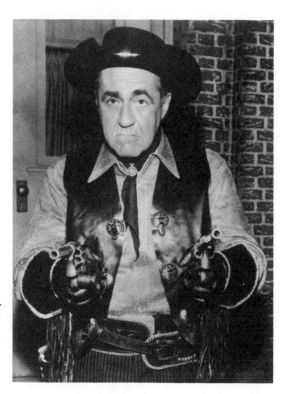

Jim Backus, on the set of "Gunsmoke" for a dream sequence in "The Sound of Quacking."
(AUTHOR'S COLLECTION)

The Skipper salivates when he sees the bird, but Gilligan befriends and protects the little duck, which he has named Everett (later realizing it's an Emily). DS: This was the first dream sequence featured in an episode. This one has Gilligan dreaming he's Marshal Gilligan, hired to protect the duck from outlaws in a western town. The scenes were actually shot on the "Gunsmoke" set. W: Lawrence J. Cohen and Fred Freeman, D: Ray Montgomery.

8. GOODBYE ISLAND   The Professor tries to make nails from an outcropping of ferrous oxide he has discovered on the island. His nails are too limp, but Gilligan and Mary Ann discover tree sap (intended for pancake syrup) that bonds like glue. The sap turns out to bond only temporarily. W: Albert E. Lewin and Burt Styler, D: John Rich.

> PROFESSOR: Well, that glue is permanent! There's nothing on the island to dissolve it. Why, do you know what it would take? It would take a polyester derivative of an organic hydroxide molecule.
> MR. HOWELL: Watch your language! You're in the presence of a lady!

9. THE BIG GOLD STRIKE   While the Castaways prepare to exit the island on the *Minnow*'s inflatable life raft, Gilligan discovers a gold mine on the island when he falls into a cavernous pit. Mr. Howell stakes a claim and has Gilligan mine it for him. All of the Castaways become greedy and eventually stow away bags of gold on the raft, which sinks in the lagoon. W: Roland Wolpert, D: Stanley Z. Cherry.

10. WAITING FOR WATUBI   Skipper unearths an ancient tiki god he recognizes as Kona and feels sure he has been cursed because of the discovery. Only the witch doctor, Watubi, can remove the curse, so Gilligan dresses up and performs the ritual to break the spell. W: Lawrence J. Cohen and Fred Freeman, D: Jack Arnold.

11. ANGEL ON THE ISLAND   Ginger is distraught when she misses her Broadway debut because they are shipwrecked. To console her, the Castaways put on the play *Cleopatra*, and Mr. Howell becomes the production's angel, or backer. Temperaments prevent the production from going well. W: Herbert Finn and Alan Dinehart, D: Jack Arnold, GC: Mel Blanc, the famous cartoon voice-characterizationist who spoke for Bugs Bunny, Daffy Duck, Barney Rubble, and hundreds more, provided the vocals for the parrot at the end of the episode.

12. BIRDS GOTTA FLY, FISH GOTTA TALK   This is the only Christmas-theme episode we filmed. Through flashbacks (including much of the original pilot film), the audience finds out exactly what happened when the S.S. *Minnow* was wrecked. The title comes from the fact that a fish swallowed the radio when Gilligan accidentally cast the transistor out to sea.

Blooper: Look very closely at the people who are sleeping on the *Minnow*'s outer deck when Gilligan wakes up. It is clearly the original Professor, Ginger, and Mary Ann from the pilot. W: Sherwood Schwartz, Elroy Schwartz, and Austin Kalish, D: Rod Amateau (original pilot footage) and John Rich (new footage).

13. THREE MILLION DOLLARS MORE OR LESS   Mr. Howell bets Gilligan, starting with a twenty-five-cent wager. Within forty-eight hours it has swelled to $3 million, which Mr. Howell owes Gilligan. Mr. Howell tries to unload a supposedly worthless oil company, but a radio report states it is a gusher. W: Bill Davenport and Charles Tannen, D: Ray Montgomery.

14. WATER, WATER EVERYWHERE   While the island is going through a drought, Gilligan manages to waste every bit of water that has been saved. The parched Castaways ration and even try a divining rod until a frog leads Gilligan to a fresh-water underground spring. Note: The "Ribbot" of the frog was supplied by cartoon voice-man and actor Mel Blanc. W: Tom and Frank Waldman, D: Stanley Z. Cherry.

Skipper holding our basic food staple on the island. (PHOTO BY GABI RONA)

15. SO SORRY, MY ISLAND NOW   A Japanese soldier who thinks World War II never ended arrives on the island in a one-man submarine and captures the Castaways. Note: This was one of those episodes that we filmed when the water in the lagoon was ice-cold. If you look closely at Bob Denver's red rugby shirt, his collar is unusually buttoned all the way up to conceal the wet suit he's wearing underneath. You can even see the zipper seam of the wet suit running from his stomach to his neck. W: David P. Harmon, D: Alan Crosland, Jr., GC: Vito Scotti (Japanese soldier).

16. PLANT YOU NOW, DIG YOU LATER   Mr. Howell claims that the treasure chest Gilligan found while working for him becomes Howell property. The Professor settles the matter by holding court and becoming the judge. The ruling: Share and share alike— it's community property. Mr. Howell offers each Castaway $100,000 for their portion and finds out the chest is filled with old cannonballs. W: Elroy Schwartz and Oliver Crawford, D: Lawrence Dobkin.

17. LITTLE ISLAND, BIG GUN   Gangster Jackson Farrell and his accomplices arrive on the island by boat. They're planning to

Vito Scotti played a Japanese soldier who didn't know the war was over. (COURTESY OF VITO SCOTTI)

hide the money from a bank they robbed, but the sack of dough ends up getting chewed up in the propeller of their boat. W: Dick Conway and Roland MacLane, D: Abner Biberman, GC: Larry Storch (Farrell), Jack Sheldon (Lucky), K. L. Smith (Gates), Louis Quinn (Hank).

18. X MARKS THE SPOT The air force drops an experimental missile on the island in a strategic test called "Operation Powder Keg." W: Sherwood Schwartz and Elroy Schwartz, D: Jack Arnold, GC: Russell Thorson (General Bryan), Harry Lauter (Major Adams).

19. GILLIGAN MEETS JUNGLE BOY Yet another inhabitant of the island turns up when Gilligan finds a jungle boy who doesn't know how to speak a language. The jungle boy shows the Professor a natural gas opening in the earth that will fill the hot-air balloon they build from sealed raincoats. W: Al Schwartz (Sherwood's other brother), Howard Merrill, and Howard Harris, D: Lawrence Dobkin, GC: Kurt Russell (Jungle Boy). Note: Sherwood Schwartz relished the fact that about ten years later an actual news report described a group of Soviet dissidents who successfully defected by similarly navigating a hot-air balloon made of raincoats.

20. ST. GILLIGAN AND THE DRAGON The women protest, then vacate the community hut when the men don't keep their promise to build private residences. The men decide to drive the women back by dressing up as a dragon and scaring them from their primitive camp. W: Arnold and Lois Peyser, D: Ray Montgomery.

21. BIG MAN ON LITTLE STICK Beefy Duke Williams rides a giant tsunami to the island. He recovers on the island and works out before he rides the tsunami back to Hawaii, but wipes out and hits his head, which causes amnesia. W: Charles Tannen and Lou Huston, D: Tony Leader, GC: Denny Scott Miller (Williams).

22. DIAMONDS ARE AN APE'S BEST FRIEND A gorilla on the island who is enchanted by Mrs. Howell's jewels and perfume

The Castaways construct a hot-air balloon out of raincoats and the friendly jungle boy is launched to civilization. (PERSONALITY PHOTOS, INC.)

steals them and then kidnaps her. W: Elroy Schwartz, D: Jack Arnold. Note: Stuntman Janos Prohaska was in the ape costume in this one.

23. HOW TO BE A HERO   When Gilligan is unable to save Mary Ann from drowning in the lagoon, Skipper jumps in and saves both of them. Skipper becomes the resident hero, and Gilligan becomes insatiably jealous. The others devise a way to make Gilligan a hero, but when he actually saves them from a headhunter, they really believe he is a hero. W: Herbert Finn and Alan Dinehart, D: Tony Leader.

24. THE RETURN OF WRONGWAY FELDMAN   The Castaways are revisited by eccentric aviator Wrongway Feldman, who

Thurston: *Now the first thing you use, darling, is your driver.*
Lovey: *My driver? Don't be silly, darling, you know perfectly well my chauffeur is back home. I believe his name was Charles, wasn't it?*
Thurston: *No, darling, I'm talking about clubs.*
Lovey: *Of course, he drove us to all the very best clubs.*
(PHOTO BY GABI RONA)

wants nothing more to do with civilization. The Castaways are distraught and try to force him to fly back to the mainland and form a rescue mission for them. Wrongway takes off and leaves them high and dry. W: Fred Freeman and Lawrence J. Cohen, D: Ida Lupino, GC: Hans Conried (Feldman).

25. THE MATCHMAKER   Mrs. Howell misses the year's social events and weddings, so she decides to engineer a romance between Gilligan and Mary Ann. The plan backfires and ends up nearly breaking up the Howells' marriage. The rest of the Castaways reunite the Howells with a romantic dinner and entertainment courtesy of Ginger. Blooper: In previous episodes, the Professor's home-made, hand-cranked record player was used, but, suddenly, a modern turntable has mysteriously appeared—or washed ashore without explanation. W: Joanna Lee, D: Tony Leader.

26. MUSIC HATH CHARM   The Castaways form an orchestra for fun, but Gilligan's drums attract angry native tribes from other islands who think his drumbeats mean war. W: Al Schwartz and Howard Harris, D: Jack Arnold, GC: Frank Corsentino, Russ Grieve, and Paul Daniel (main natives).

27. NEW NEIGHBOR SAM   The Castaways are petrified when they overhear voices of gangsters who are threatening to kill them. It turns out that the "voices" belong to a parrot speaking in two different voices. W: Charles Tannen and George O'Hanlon, D: Ray Montgomery, GC: The voices of the parrot were those of Mel Blanc and Herb Vigran.

28. THEY'RE OFF AND RUNNING   After turtle racing, Mr. Howell wins everything Skipper owns, including Gilligan. Howell wants Gilligan to be his permanent houseboy.

During the filming of this episode, the animal trainers had several turtles they stored in Bob Denver's dressing-room shower when they weren't on camera. Bob retreated to his dressing room one evening and was surprised that there were turtles in there soaking. W: Walter Black, D: Jack Arnold.

29. THREE TO GET READY   Gilligan finds a rare gemstone that Skipper is convinced is the "Eye of the Idol." According to its legend, Gilligan is granted three wishes. He wastes the first two on gallons of ice cream that mysteriously float ashore. The Professor says this is coincidental. Gilligan finally expends his last chance and wishes the Castaways "off the island." The patch of land they're standing on separates into the lagoon. W: David P. Harmon, D: Jack Arnold.

30. FORGET ME NOT   Skipper is struck on the head and suffers paranoid delusions. He thinks the Castaways are Japanese soldiers out to get him. The Professor has to hypnotize Skipper to snap him out of it, but only after a rescue plane has flown over the island. W: Herbert Margolis, D: Jack Arnold.

31. DIOGENES, WON'T YOU PLEASE GO HOME?   Everyone finds out about the diary that Gilligan is keeping. He's recording the events of their day-to-day life stuck together. Flashbacks reveal everyone's own version of how he or she escaped the Japanese soldier a while back. W: David P. Harmon, D: Christian Nyby, GC: Vito Scotti (Japanese soldier).

32. PHYSICAL FATNESS   From the chemicals available on the island, the Professor is able to concoct a phosphorescent dye marker for the Castaways to signal for help. Meanwhile, the Skipper goes on a diet to lose poundage and Gilligan tries to gain weight by eating everything in sight, including the Professor's dye. W: Herbert Finn and Alan Dinehart, D: Gary Nelson.

33. IT'S MAGIC   A huge crate of magician's props has washed up in the lagoon. The Castaways test them, and Gilligan screws up every attempt at prestidigitation. W: Al Schwartz and Bruce Howard, D: Jack Arnold.

34. GOODBYE, OLD PAINT   The Castaways discover yet another person on the island: famous abstract painter Alexandri Gregor Dubov. They find out that the lazy Dubov owns a short-wave radio, but won't let anyone use it to call for help. The Castaways scheme to make Dubov jealous of Gilligan's artistic talent, so he will yearn to go home. Dubov indeed becomes jealous and flees the island on a raft he has made from his paintings. W: David P. Harmon, D: Jack Arnold, GC: Harold J. Stone (Dubov).

35. MY FAIR GILLIGAN (DS)   Mr. and Mrs. Howell are so grateful that Gilligan saved Lovey's life that they decide to adopt him as a Howell. Gilligan dreams that he has become a mean prince, the son of King Thurston and Queen Lovey. Gilligan wakes up and realizes he hates being a Howell and tries to go back to being just

Skipper begins to see things in "Forget Me Not." (AUTHOR'S COLLECTION)

plain first mate. W: Joanna Lee, D: Tony Leader, GC: Tom Forstor (Executioner).

36. A NOSE BY ANY OTHER NAME Gilligan nearly breaks his nose when he falls out of a tree and is convinced he requires an operation to fix it. The Professor pretends to operate on Gilligan and give him a nose job in the same procedure. W: Elroy Schwartz, D: Hal Cooper.

37. GILLIGAN'S MOTHER-IN-LAW This was the first episode filmed in color. This second-season premiere is about a fat native girl and her parents who visit the island. The native girl wants to marry Gilligan, which would mean a trip to another island, but Gilligan chickens out. Note: Jim Backus's wife, Henny, plays the stubborn mother of the well-rounded native girl. W: Budd Grossman, D: Jack Arnold, GC: Russ Grieve (Chief), Henny Backus (Mother), Mary Foran (Daughter), Eddie Little Sky (Haruki, the native).

38. BEAUTY IS AS BEAUTY DOES Who is the most beautiful woman on the island? The Professor emcees a beauty pageant, and all the men choose sides and sabotage the competition. Since Gilligan has no favorite, both sides try to bribe him into casting the deciding vote their way. Instead, Gilligan chooses Gladys, the monkey, as Miss Deserted Isle, since she is the only true native of the island. W: Joanna Lee, D: Jack Arnold.

39. THE LITTLE DICTATOR (DS) Pancho Hernando Gonzales Enrico Rodriguez, the exiled President of the Republic of Equarico, is placed on the island with a firing squad. He attempts to rule the Castaways with his gun.

Gilligan dreams that he is a dictator who promises his nation "dis, dat and the other ting," but then realizes he is nothing but a puppet ruler. He wakes up to find the dictator fleeing the island with the firing squad. Note: This is Sherwood Schwartz's favorite episode. W: Bob Rodgers and Sid Mandel, D: Jack Arnold, GC: Nehemiah Persoff (Rodriguez), Bert Madrid (José).

Mary Foran was a native girl from another island who wanted to marry Gilligan. (PERSONALITY PHOTOS, INC.)

*Henny Backus (Jim's wife) played a native in "Gilligan's Mother-in-Law,"
our first episode in color.* (COURTESY OF HENNY BACKUS)

40. SMILE, YOU'RE ON MARS CAMERA   One of NASA's satellites, with a television camera mounted on it, lands on the island. Gilligan breaks the camera's lens, and the Professor repairs it. At Cape Canaveral, the scientists assume the craft has landed on Mars. Through a mishap, NASA only sees the Castaways covered with feathers that Gilligan has collected. W: Al Schwartz and Bruce Howard, D: Jack Arnold, GC: Booth Coleman, Larry Thor, Arthur Peterson (scientists).

41. THE SWEEPSTAKES (DS)   A radio broadcast reveals that Gilligan owns the winning lotto number in a South American sweepstakes. The Howells allow him to join their private country club, and Gilligan obtains membership for the remaining Castaways as well.

Mr. Howell is furious, but learns his lesson when he dreams he is a grizzled, old Magoo-like prospector who has come down from the hills on his donkey, Sea Biscuit. The prospector carries a sack full of gold, which he shares with others in a western town.

"The Sweepstakes" was Jim Backus's favorite episode. In a dream, Marshal Gilligan tries to protect an old prospector and his million dollars in gold.
(PERSONALITY PHOTOS, INC.)

Note: This episode, which again made use of the "Gunsmoke" set for a background, was Jim Backus's favorite show. W: Walter Black, D: Jack Arnold.

42. QUICK BEFORE IT SINKS   The Professor thinks the island is sinking rapidly and throws the rest of the Castaways into a panic. They decide to build a gigantic ark to float off the sinking island. It ends up that Gilligan has been moving the Professor's measuring stick and the whole panic was for nothing. W: Stan Burns and Mike Marmer, D: George Cahan.

43. CASTAWAYS PICTURES PRESENTS   This remains one of the most popular of all the episodes because of its sheer ridiculousness. In this one the Castaways discover crates in the hull of a sunken ship at the bottom of the lagoon that are filled with costumes, motion picture cameras, makeup, and other film paraphernalia.

Mr. Howell directs a silent epic that hilariously explains their plight, but they hope it will instigate a rescue after they set the film adrift. Instead, the film is found and heralded as a possible lost work of Ingmar Bergman and given first place at the Cannes Film Festival. W: Herbert Finn and Alan Dinehart, D: Jack Arnold.

44. AGONIZED LABOR   According to radio reports, Howell Industries has gone under and the couple is bankrupt. The Castaways pitch in to teach the Howells some kind of trade, since they have never worked at anything but being wealthy. Just as the Howells decide to commit suicide, another radio report announces that it was actually *Powell* Industries that had gone belly-up. W: Roland Mac-Lane, D: Jack Arnold.

45. NYET, NYET—NOT YET   A Soviet space capsule lands on the island and the two Russian cosmonauts attempt to leave the island without the Castaways. Paranoia spreads as the Russians think the Castaways are spies and the Castaways think the cosmonauts have ulterior motives. The Cosmonauts are rescued by a submarine, leaving the Castaways still stranded. W: Adele T. Strassfield and Robert Riordan, D: Jack Arnold, GC: Danny Klega (Ivan), Vincent Beck (Igor).

46. HI-FI GILLIGAN   Gilligan becomes a human radio receiver when Skipper accidentally knocks him in the face with a crate. (Really, it was an accident!) A typhoon approaches the island, and when the regular radio breaks, Gilligan becomes the source for weather updates. W: Mary C. McCall, D: Jack Arnold.

47. THE CHAIN OF COMMAND   Skipper tries to prepare his protégé, Gilligan, to be prepared for anything in case he must take charge in an emergency. Skipper disappears to test Gilligan's abilities. W: Arnold and Lois Peyser, D: Leslie Goodwins.

48. DON'T BUG THE MOSQUITOES   Some viewers consider this episode one of the best. A rock group called the Mosquitoes lands on the island for some relaxation, but the Castaways try to make them return to the mainland. Both the men and the women Castaways form singing trios, hoping to encourage the Mosquitoes to depart early. The plan backfires. The visiting rock band is intimidated by the girls' group, the Honeybees, and departs the island, leaving a gift: a copy of their album, *The Mosquitoes Live at Carnegie Hall.* Note: Three of the Mosquitoes (Patterson, Wade, and Johnson) were actually the three singers known as the Wellingtons, who sang the first season's theme song. W: Brad Radnitz, D: Steve Binder, GC: Les Brown, Jr. (Bingo), George Patterson (Bango), Ed Wade (Bongo), Kirby Johnson (Irving).

49. GILLIGAN GETS BUGGED   Gilligan has been bitten by what the Professor says is a poisonous Mantis Carni bug. Eventually, they all get bitten. The Castaways search for the proper ingredients so the Professor can prepare an antidote, but the bug ends up being harmless. W: Jack Gross, Jr., and Michael R. Stein, D: Gary Nelson.

50. MINE HERO   While fishing in the lagoon, Gilligan hauls in a World War II mine, which panics the Castaways. The Professor fails to deactivate the mine, so Gilligan tows it out into the lagoon, where it detonates, harming no one. W: David Braverman and Bob Marcus, D: Wilbur D'Arcy.

51. ERIKA TIFFANY SMITH TO THE RESCUE   Wealthy socialite Erika Tiffany Smith, an old acquaintance of the Howells', arrives on the island in search of two things: a spot to build a resort hotel and a husband. She falls for the Professor, who is too busy cataloging flora and fauna to understand how to encourage a romantic relationship. When Erika departs, she promises to send help for the Castaways, only there is a storm, and she can't relocate the tiny island. W: David P. Harmon, D: Jack Arnold, GC: Zsa Zsa Gabor (Erika), Michael Whitney (Erika's assistant, Johnny).

52. NOT GUILTY   No matter how much time passes, nearly every bit of media news that reaches the Castaways is about them in some way. This time, Gilligan hauls in from the lagoon a crate with old Honolulu newspapers inside. One newspaper article indicates that the crew and passengers aboard the S.S. *Minnow* are being sought in a murder investigation. The Castaways become suspicious of each other, and finally, in an effort to solve the Randolph Blake murder case, the Castaways re-create the events of the night before they sailed. W: Roland MacLane, D: Stanley Z. Cherry.

53. YOU'VE BEEN DISCONNECTED   A telephone line washes up on the lagoon, and the Professor manages to break into the giant cable and rig up a telephone so they can dial out for help. Each attempt at reaching a long-distance line is futile. A storm hits and pulls the cable back out to sea. W: Elroy Schwartz, D: Jack Arnold, GC: Redheaded Sandra Gould, better known as Gladys Kravitz, the nosy neighbor on "Bewitched," plays a terse telephone operator.

54. THE POSTMAN COMETH (DS)   It seems that Mary Ann has been sending notes in a bottle to her old boyfriend back home.

Coincidentally, Gilligan turns on the radio and hears that her boy-friend (Horace Higgenbotham *from Kansas*) has already wed. Through a misunderstanding, Mary Ann eavesdrops on a conversation and assumes she's dying from the mushrooms she's eaten. That night, she dreams she is in a hospital room and crazy nurses and doctors visit her. The Professor is like a Dr. Cary Grant, who enters the wacky hospital room and diagnoses Mary Ann with "roomus degloomus."

Mary Ann admits she had been lying about a boyfriend the whole time and was just trying to make the others think there was someone special back home waiting for her. W: Herbert Finn and Alan Dinehart, D: Leslie Goodwins.

55. SEER GILLIGAN   Gilligan can read minds thanks to some special seeds he discovered on the island. Everybody gets hold of the powerful seeds and finds out the others' true thoughts. This leads to disaster when everyone insults each other through their honesty. Gilligan solves the problem by burning the bush that bore the seeds. W: Elroy Schwartz, D: Leslie Goodwins.

56. LOVE ME, LOVE MY SKIPPER   Mr. Howell accidentally loses Skipper's invitation to the Howell cotillion, and the rest of the Castaways assume the Howells meant to exclude him. They decide to boycott the cotillion and throw a costume party in honor of the Skipper, which causes a spat between the Howells. After the bash, which Gilligan literally crashes as Tarzan on a vine, all animosities are forgotten. W: Herbert Finn and Alan Dinehart, D: Tony Leader.

57. GILLIGAN'S LIVING DOLL   A silver robot, which Skipper calls "a refugee from *The Wizard of Oz*," parachutes onto the island, and the Professor attempts to program it to rescue the Castaways by walking ("one hundred eleven hours") to Hawaii. The robot reaches Hawaii, but through a radio report, the Castaways find out the programmed message had been scrambled by Gilligan's rabbit's foot, which he jammed into the robot for good luck. W: Bob Stevens, D: Leslie Goodwins, GC: Bob D'Arcy was inside the robot, and Charles Maxwell spoke for the Tin Man.

Skipper becomes a pirate for the island costume party. (PERSONALITY PHO-
TOS, INC.)

58. FORWARD MARCH   The Castaways think they are being
attacked when live hand grenades and gunfire rake the ground
around them. They go into an intensive army drill and prepare for
war and casualties, then discover the gorilla that's been randomly
activating the arsenal of weaponry hidden in a cave. W: Jack Raymond, D: Jerry Hopper.

59. SHIP AHOAX   Fearing that the isolation is about to drive
everyone crazy, the Professor pulls a scam with Ginger, who pretends to be a psychic predicting a rescue in order to lift everyone's
spirits. Ginger holds a séance and reveals the scheme to everyone.
W: Charles Tannen and George O'Hanlon, D: Leslie Goodwins.

60. FEED THE KITTY   A crate containing a lion headed for a zoo accidentally gets misdirected and washes up on the lagoon. Gilligan removes a thorn from the temperamental beast, and the two become pals. When the Castaways run out of lion food, Gilligan thinks the lion has consumed the Skipper. W: J. E. Selby and Dick Sanville, D: Leslie Goodwins.

61. OPERATION: STEAM HEAT   The earth's temperature is rising. The Professor speculates that there is underground volcanic activity on the island, so he searches for materials to construct a nitroglycerine bomb that will spike the volcano on the other side of the island. (The Professor's ingredients for the bomb include sulfuric acid from the crystalized copper in the caves, glycerol from papaya seeds, and potassium nitrate from rocks in the lagoon.) The bomb works, the volcanic eruption is reversed. Again, the Professor saves their lives. W: Terence and Joan Maples, D: Stanley Z. Cherry.

62. WILL THE REAL MR. HOWELL PLEASE STAND UP?   At this point, I think the writers of our show began feeling the effects of island fever. We all thought this one really came out of left field.

The radio announcer reports that Thurston Howell has returned to civilization and is doing big business. Obviously, there is an imposter who is spending the Howell fortune. The real Thurston is frantic! Ready to kill!

The Castaways all try to devise an immediate means of returning Mr. Howell to civilization. Gilligan builds huge wings and leaps off the hut's thatched roof, hovering for a few moments—until Skipper tells him he can't fly. Note: Out of desperation, the real Thurston Howell decides to head out to sea on a pontoon. The Professor hands him the ship's flare gun for emergency, despite the fact that Gilligan wasted the last flare episodes ago!

The phony Howell somehow happens to coincidentally land on the island and konks the real Howell on his head and masquerades as the millionaire. Even Lovey can't tell who is who. W: Bud Grossman, D: Jack Arnold.

63. GHOST À GO-GO   Gilligan sees a ghost, then Mary Ann and Ginger witness an apparition haunting the island. The ghost informs the Castaways that they must leave in the boat he has provided.

The Professor is suspicious of the ploy, so the Castaways construct dummies of themselves to put aboard the boat. The boat blows up in the water, and the Castaways find out that it is a spy who has been running around in the white sheets. Then they pretend to be ghosts and roam around in white sheets and howl, scaring the spy off the island. W: Roland MacLane, D: Leslie Goodwins, GC: Richard Kiel (Ghost), Charles Maxwell (voice on the walkie-talkie).

64. ALLERGY TIME   Skipper can't stop itching and sneezing when he's around Gilligan, and the Professor determines that he is allergic to his little buddy. Gilligan tries to move in with the Howells, and then the girls, and finally the Professor—but everyone throws him out.

Everyone is allergic to Gilligan. The Professor develops a vaccine that he injects into the Castaways with a giant hypodermic needle, but it does no good. The problem all along was the oil from the papaya nuts used in Gilligan's hair tonic. W: Budd Grossman, D: Jack Arnold.

65. THE FRIENDLY PHYSICIAN   Crazed scientist Dr. Boris Balinkoff arrives on the island and takes the Castaways back to his laboratory on another island. There he experiments by switching the mind of one person with another. He exchanges Gilligan's mind with Mr. Howell's body, and Mrs. Howell's mind with Skipper's. Mary Ann and the Professor are transposed. And Ginger and Balinkoff's goon, Igor, are mind-melded. Note: This is the only episode in which the Castaways leave the island, but they return in a boat. But the boat sinks in the lagoon before they are able to head back to Hawaii. W: Elroy Schwartz, D: Jack Arnold, GC: Vito Scotti (Balinkoff), Mike Mazurki (Igor).

66. "V" FOR VITAMINS (DS)   There is a vitamin deficiency on the island because of a lack of citrus fruit, and only one orange remains. The Castaways plant the orange's seeds, and while Gilligan keeps vigil over them so they don't die in the cold night air, he dreams he is Jack from "Jack in the Beanstalk," scaling the vine up to a giant's castle.

The Professor finds a citrus grove of lemons and grapefruits on the other side of the island. Gilligan knew about them all the time, only he didn't realize lemons and grapefruit were citrus fruit. W: Barney Slater, D: Jack Arnold, GC: Patrick Denver, Bob's son, plays the little Gilligan in the dream sequence.

67. MR. AND MRS.???   A radio report reveals that the minister who married Thurston and Lovey (Reverend Buckley Norris of Boston) was a fraud and the Howells' marriage is null and void. The Howells decide to remarry in the lagoon, with Skipper presiding over the ceremony.

The wedding is a disaster. Thurston and Lovey argue, and finally separate. The Castaways try to reunite the feuding couple by making them jealous. The Professor takes Mrs. Howell out on a date the same evening that Ginger and Mr. Howell are out on the town together. As it turns out, the radio announcer was at fault. He mispronounced the minister's name. It was Boris Nuckley who performed invalid marriages, not Buckley Norris. W: Jack Gross, Jr., and Michael R. Stein, D: Gary Nelson.

68. MEET THE METEOR (DS)   A large, glowing meteorite lands on the island. The Professor investigates and detects strong cosmic rays with his bamboo Geiger counter. So the men fit themselves with protective lead costumes and makeup and build a shield that surrounds the meteorite. The result is that the fallen chunk of meteor ages things around it drastically. Later, Gilligan dreams the Castaways are old and doddering when they celebrate their fiftieth anniversary on the island with a big party.

Gilligan saves this one. When he wakes up, he finds himself outside in the middle of a storm. He hurls a lead lightning rod into the meteor, which attracts a bolt that destroys the unwanted rock. W: Elroy Schwartz, D: Jack Arnold.

Little Patrick Denver played a miniature version of his dad in a dream sequence. (AUTHOR'S COLLECTION)

69. UP AT BAT (DS)   This third-season opener is one of the most memorable of the bunch in my opinion. In this "Dracula" episode Gilligan is bitten by a flying bat and goes berserk because he's afraid he will become a vampire. He hides out in a cave and has a nightmare that he is Count Dracula, Ginger is his wife, a Vampira dressed in shrouds, and Mary Ann is the old-hag keeper of the English inn where the story takes place. Dracula attacks the Howells, and Inspector Sherlock and his assistant, Watney (Professor and Skipper), burst onto the scene and punch out the vampires in a "Kapow! Boff!" wink at TV's "Batman." The Professor finally catches the bat flapping in the girls' hut and calms everyone down:

> "Hold it! . . . Now listen to me. This is not Gilligan, and it's not a vampire bat. It's a perfectly understandable mistake. Now this is a common red fruit bat. It's perfectly harmless. However, it can be mistaken for the vampire bat. Only an expert can tell them apart and fortunately I happen to know a little something about bat anatomy."

W: Ron Friedman, D: Jerry Hopper.

70. GILLIGAN VS. GILLIGAN   Another Castaway hybrid visits the island. This time, a Russian spy who has undergone plastic surgery to resemble Gilligan steals Mary Ann's pies and pretends to be the first mate. When Gilligan denies it, the Professor confronts him:

> PROFESSOR: On the basis of circumstantial evidence, I'm afraid you're a prevaricator.
> GILLIGAN: Well, that's better than calling me a liar.

Gilligan finally meets his twin, but cannot convince anyone else that his double, who holds a shiny gold pocketknife, is on the island. The Professor concludes that Gilligan is going through a psychological crisis. The treatment: Humor the poor stupe. W: Joanna Lee, D: Jerry Hopper.

As Inspector Sherlock in the
vampire dream sequence.
(AUTHOR'S COLLECTION)

71. PASS THE VEGETABLES PLEASE With this script, we thought we'd seen it all.

Gilligan fishes a crate of radioactive vegetable seeds from the lagoon, and all of the Castaways are excited about starting a garden of new taste treats. When they plant the seeds, they are amazed at how quickly and grossly misshapen the vegetables grew. They consume the freak veggies anyway, in a gluttonous dinner feast.

All of a sudden, the Castaways possess superhuman strengths and abilities, which they don't know are provided by the radioactive seeds. Thanks to the spinach, Gilligan lifts heavy tree trunks effortlessly. Mary Ann gobbles a dish of carrots that increases her vision to such extraordinary dimensions that she spots a ship with a lot of sailors many miles out at sea.

MARY ANN: Oh, won't it be wonderful when those sailors pick us up, Ginger?

GINGER: Won't be the first time it's happened to me, Mary Ann.

Mrs. Howell runs around as if she is on speed, a side effect of the sugar beets she keeps shoveling in. (Even after she has learned they are dangerous, she keeps eating them because they are her favorite.)

When the Castaways learn the food is radioactive, the Professor counteracts the effect by making everyone consume large and strong amounts of their homemade soap, which contains hydrocarbons that absorb the vegetables' radioactivity. W: Elroy Schwartz, D: Leslie Goodwins.

72. THE PRODUCER　Most kids are introduced to the superb comic talent of Phil Silvers through this episode, which involves Harold Hecuba, the famous Hollywood producer, who lands on the island during his worldwide talent search. The cigar-chomping egomaniac orders the Castaways around and demands that the Howells relinquish their accommodations. Eventually, the Howells stoop to becoming Hecuba's butler and maid.

The Castaways attempt to put on a musical version of *Hamlet* to showcase Ginger's talents and force Hecuba to whisk her back to Hollywood. "Neither a borrower nor a lender be . . . Do not forget: stay out of debt." They rehearse secretly at night, but Hecuba is awakened and takes over the whole production. Later, he vanishes, and through a radio report the Castaways find out that he is planning to introduce to the world his monumental musical version of *Hamlet*. W: Gerald Gardner and Dee Caruso, D: Ida Lupino, GC: Phil Silvers (Hecuba).

73. VOODOO A lot of fans have told me this is the best episode. Strange things begin to happen to the Castaways just about the time they all realize that their personal effects are mysteriously missing from their huts.

Scene cut: Inside a cave. A witch doctor has stolen the Castaways' items and made voodoo dolls in their likenesses to control them. He burns the bottom of their feet by torching each doll's feet.

Next, the witch doctor turns the Professor into a motionless zombie, and the other Castaways try to snap him out of it. Eventually, Gilligan stumbles upon the voodoo dolls and personal effects in the cave and hauls the stuff back to the others. The spell on the Professor has been broken, but he cannot grasp the theory of zombification.

Gilligan finally makes a voodoo doll of the witch doctor and takes vengeance with a straight pin. W: Herbert Finn and Alan Dinehart, D: George M. Cahan, GC: Eddie Little Sky (Witch Doctor).

74. WHERE THERE'S A WILL Mr. Howell revises his will, leaving each of the Castaways a nice chunk of his estate. When the Castaways decide to throw him a party to show their gratitude, he misunderstands and thinks they are trying to kill him to collect their inheritance.

Howell becomes more convinced that he's being stalked when he overhears the Castaways planning to "cut the pig's throat." (They're actually trapping a wild boar to prepare him some spareribs.) Howell moves to the other side of the island for protection and almost sinks in quicksand. The others find his hat atop the quicksand and assume he has died. Howell witnesses his own funeral, is impressed by the service, and sees that his "widow" and his friends are genuinely grief-stricken. W: Sid Mandel and Roy Kammerman, D: Charles Norton.

75. MAN WITH A NET Lord Beasley Waterford, a famous butterfly collector, is on the island to capture the world's rarest specimen, a pussycat swallowtail. The desperate Castaways try everything but murder in an effort to make him fire his flare as a signal for a rescue boat on a nearby island. They even try to get

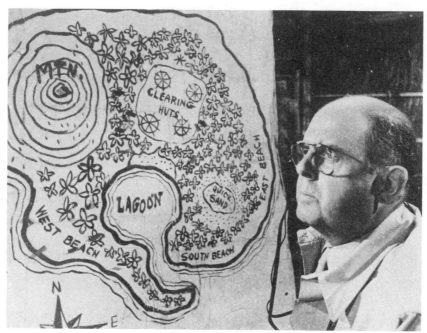

John McGiver played Lord Beasley Waterford, who visits the island in search of a rare butterfly known as the pussycat swallowtail. (COURTESY OF SHERWOOD SCHWARTZ)

Beasley drunk on fermented island fruit, but end up passing out themselves while he remains sober.

Eventually, the butterfly nut joins the ranks of the other jerks who have left the island and told no one of the shipwrecked seven. W: Budd Grossman, D: Leslie Goodwins, GC: John McGiver (Waterford).

76. HAIR TODAY, GONE TOMORROW This episode is simple, but hilarious: Gilligan wakes up one morning suffering from "follicular albinism"—his hair has gone white. He thinks he's aging drastically and gathers the "children" around his rocking chair to divide his belongings among them. He leaves his body to the Professor.

Mrs. Howell attempts to dye Gilligan's hair brown in the middle of the night, and the next morning Gilligan discovers he has lost all of his hair. Bald Gilligan is ashamed to face the others, so he runs away and resides in a cave. Skipper also goes bald and joins Gilligan in the hideaway. The Castaways lure them out of the cave by providing them George and Martha Washington wigs that the Howells just happen to have brought along. The Professor finally deduces that the crude bleach Gilligan and Skipper were using to wash everyone's clothing has caused all the problems.

Mrs. Howell's famous breakfast order: "I think I'll have a hard-bald egg."

W: Brad Radnitz, D: Tony Leader.

77. RING AROUND GILLIGAN   Mad scientist Boris Balinkoff makes a return visit to the island with his monkey. This time, Balinkoff can command the Castaways when they wear a ring that places them under his hypnotic trance. He begins working them as robots and sabotaging their own rescue raft until his transmitter is broken by flying coconuts. W: John Fenton Murray, D: George M. Cahan, GC: Vito Scotti (Balinkoff).

Skipper: "Oh, no, Professor, if you've got my hairs, I never want to see 'em again. They're deserters." (COURTESY OF MRS. ALAN HALE, JR.)

78. TOPSY-TURVY   Amidst a continual beat of native drums, Gilligan is struck on the skull once again and sees everything upside down. The Professor brews an antidote made of keptibora berry extract, which causes Gilligan to see double. With more juice, he sees four of everything. Headhunters invade the island and capture all the Castaways except Gilligan, who saves the day by feeding the natives the keptibora berry juice.

Blooper: Look at the establishing shot of the natives' bamboo prison and you'll notice there are a few walls missing. W: Elroy Schwartz, D: Gary Nelson, GC: Eddie Little Sky, Roman Gabriel, Allen Jaffe.

79. THE INVASION (DS)   This episode was our answer to James Bond, "Get Smart," and Inspector Clouseau all rolled into one bizarre dream.

While fishing, Gilligan hooks an attaché case with the words "Property of U.S. Government" stamped on it. The Professor becomes outrageously paranoid and refuses to let anyone inspect the contents for fear the materials within are top secret; that night, the Castaways are so inquisitive about the briefcase they individually try stealing it from the Professor's hut.

Gilligan accidentally handcuffs himself to the attaché case and the next night dreams he is Secret Agent 014 in a spy adventure in which he must deliver the booby-trapped attaché case. Mary Ann is EVIL Agent 10, who speaks to her EVIL leader, a bald Mr. Howell. Ginger is EVIL Agent 5, who speaks to Howell through a soup ladle and attempts to get rid of good-guy Agent 014 with a poisonous kiss. But Agent 014 lives because he's wearing his peel-off Lipgard. Later, the Skipper is EVIL Agent 1, who looks like Jonathan Winters's Maude Frickert, and pretends to be Agent 014's mother.

It ends up that the attaché case contains useless World War I documents. W: Sam Locke and Joel Rapp; D: Leslie Goodwins.

80. THE KIDNAPPER   Mrs. Howell, Mary Ann, and Ginger are successively kidnapped for ransom money. The kidnapper, Norbert Wiley, is caught and interrogated. He's a compulsive gambler who

In "The Invasion," Gilligan dreams he is a secret agent; Skipper is not his mother, but rather an evil imposter dressed like his mother. (COURTESY OF SHERWOOD SCHWARTZ)

has left civilization to avoid temptation. Wiley cons the Castaways into trusting him, and, after they are convinced he is decriminalized, they throw him a party. Wiley escapes the island with Mrs. Howell's pearl necklace, Mr. Howell's wallet, and Ginger's earrings. W: Ray Singer, D: Jerry Hopper, GC: Don Rickles (Wiley).

81. AND THEN THERE WERE NONE (DS) This is the "Jekyll and Hyde" show. Gilligan dreams he turns into a hideous monster at the mere mention of food. (The line that really does it is "Freeeeesh Fiiiish!")

One by one, the Castaways are "abducted." The Professor feels it is the work of headhunters, but, in fact, the Castaways have all fallen into an old World War II munitions pit. Gilligan turns out to be the only one on the island's surface. While searching for the others, he hears them calling him and becomes convinced they are haunting him. He backs up into a tree and knocks himself unconscious. He dreams he is called to court as Dr. Gilligan, a defendant in an old English murder trial. Mr. Howell is Judge Lord Anthony Armstrong Hanging; Mary Ann is the smudged young cockney girl; the Professor plays the prosecuting barrister; and Lovey plays Mary Poppins, the defendant's attorney. Lady Red (Ginger) reveals the secret of transforming Dr. Gilligan into a monster.

When he awakes from his stupor, Gilligan finds the others stranded in the pit. W: Ron Friedman, D: Jerry Hopper.

82. ALL ABOUT EVA   Eva Grubb, a lonely, drab woman who has left civilization seeking privacy, finds her way to the island. In an effort to lift her spirits, the women give her a total beauty make-over and Eva turns out a ravishing beauty. In fact, she's Ginger's twin.

Eva is so taken by the transformation that she konks Ginger over the head with a rock and attempts to masquerade as the movie star that night at a party. After the Castaways discover Eva's charade, she leaves the island ashamed—but she has gained enough self-confidence to assume Ginger Grant's movie career back in Hollywood. W: Joanna Lee, D: Jerry Hopper, GC: Vernon Scott (radio announcer).

83. GILLIGAN GOES GUNG-HO   Law and order is established on the island when Skipper becomes sheriff and Gilligan his deputy. Gilligan turns Barney Fife and takes his responsibility too seriously, abusing his power and eventually locking everyone up, including himself. He's cost the Castaways yet another rescue when a plane flies over the island and none of them is able to escape from the bamboo prison in time. W: Bruce Howard, D: Robert Sheerer.

84. TAKE A DARE   Bespectacled George Barkley will win $10,000 from a game show called "Take a Dare" if he's able to spend a week alone on an island fending for himself. Naturally, he's placed on our uncharted desert paradise. Items such as cooking utensils, a hammock, and other luxuries are missing from camp and Skipper and Gilligan discover the culprit: Barkley. Barkley prohibits the Castaways from communicating on his radio transmitter. It remains a mystery why he doesn't just take the money Howell offers him. W: Roland MacLane, D: Stanley Z. Cherry, GC: Strother Martin (Barkley).

85. COURT-MARTIAL (DS)   Once again, the crew of the S.S. *Minnow* is in the news. It seems the Maritime Board of Inquiry has determined that "Skipper" Jonas Grumby was at fault in the famous shipwreck. Trying to disprove the board's verdict, the Castaways reenact the shipwreck and find out the cause was Gilligan's ineptness. Skipper shares the blame with his first mate, and they exile themselves in the jungle.

That night, Gilligan has a nightmare in which he is Lord Admiral Gilligan who storms a pirate ship to free the queen mother and her two beautiful daughters.

Later, a radio report updates the situation and the Castaways find out that Skipper has been cleared of the charges. W: Roland Mac-Lane, D: Gary Nelson.

The dream-inspired Lord Admiral Gilligan, whose ship is invaded by pirate cutthroats. (PERSONALITY PHOTOS, INC.)

Rory Calhoun plays big-game hunter Jonathan Kincaid, who is on a lunatic manhunt. (PERSONALITY PHOTOS, INC.)

86. THE HUNTER Big-game hunter Jonathan Kincaid and his turbaned assistant, Ramoo, copter down to the island for sport one day. Gilligan becomes the target of Kincaid's twisted manhunt, but he manages to outrun the armed hunter.

Kincaid welches on his promise to rescue the Castaways if Gilligan escapes bullets within the twenty-four-hour limit. W: Ben Gershman and William Freedman, D: Leslie Goodwins, GC: Rory Calhoun (Kincaid), Harold Sakata (Ramoo).

87. LOVEY'S SECRET ADMIRER (DS) Lovey doesn't know who has been leaving her anonymous love notes. The Professor rigs up a lie detector using the ship's horn and batteries from the radio, but none of the men tests guilty. (Funny, they didn't test the women.) The notes remain a mystery, until they catch Mr. Howell in the act one night. Lovey demands a separation because she's been insulted.

That night, Lovey falls asleep listening to a radio narrative of the fairy tale Cinderella and dreams that she is the abused stepsister who cannot attend the ball. With the help of her fairy godfather, Gilligan,

Mr. Howell was the prince to Mrs. Howell's Cinderella in "Lovey's Secret Admirer." (PERSONALITY PHOTOS, INC.)

she goes to the ball and leaves the glass slipper just like in the story. W: Herbert Finn and Alan Dinehart, D: David McDearmon, GC: Midget Billy Curtis plays the bottom half of the knight in shining armor.

88. OUR VINES HAVE TENDER APES   Tongo, dressed in leopard loincloth, arrives on the island and tries to convince the Castaways that he's a real, uncivilized ape-man. Actually, he's an actor studying for a role. Tongo goes head-to-head with a real gorilla and cowers. Ashamed, he leaves the Castaways stranded on the island. W: Sid Mandel and Roy Kammerman, D: David McDarmon, GC: Denny Scott Miller (Tongo); stuntman Janos Prohaska is in the gorilla suit.

89. GILLIGAN'S PERSONAL MAGNETISM   A tropical lightning storm suddenly hits—right during Gilligan and Skipper's bowling tournament. Gilligan is struck by lightning, and the stone bowling ball becomes molecularly attached to him. The Professor proclaims that the ball contains iron ore and has been magnetized to Gilligan. The Howells think Gilligan's problem is psychological.

The Professor zaps the bowling ball with a generator-powered electrode and separates them, which makes Gilligan invisible. That night at dinner, Skipper reads Gilligan's runaway note, which says he's moving to the other side of the island. (The Professor asks, "Why would he do a foolish thing like that?") In time, Gilligan's invisibility wears off. W: Bruce Howard, D: Hal Cooper.

90. SPLASHDOWN According to the Professor's calculations, the orbital path of *Scorpio* 6, a newly launched space capsule, will pass right over the island. He rigs up a telegraph with the radio and hopes to make contact with the astronauts, but that elaborate scheme fails. So the Castaways try something else: They spell out SOS with flaming tree logs for the astronauts to see, but Gilligan catches fire and runs into the logs, spelling SOL instead. (Living with Gilligan, they were always SOL.)

An unmanned capsule later lands on the island, but the radio controls are damaged and the Professor can't repair them. Eventually, the capsule blows up in the middle of the lagoon just before the Castaways are about to board it and set out to sea.

Note: Watch Gilligan when he's lighting the logs. You can see his pants smoking *before* he backs up into the flaming logs. W: John Fenton Murray, D: Jerry Hopper, GC: Chick Hern (Radio commentator), George Neise (NASA official), Scott Graham (Astronaut Tobias), Jim Spencer (Astronaut Ryan).

91. HIGH MAN ON THE TOTEM POLE Gilligan and Skipper find a totem pole topped with a head that is carved in Gilligan's likeness. The Professor examines the pole and explains that it belongs to the fierce tribe of Kupaki headhunters. Gilligan becomes obsessed with the carved head and believes he *is* a headhunter.

The Kupaki headhunters find that someone has axed the "mashuka" off of the sacred totem pole, so Gilligan must dress as their native ancestor to drive the Kupaki off the island. W: Brad Radnitz, D: Herbert Coleman, GC: Jim Lefebvre, Al Ferrara, Pete Sotos (Kupaki headhunters).

92. THE SECOND GINGER GRANT This is the "amnesia" episode, in which Mary Ann tries imitating Ginger by singing "I Wanna Be Loved by You." Mary Ann falls backward while watching one of Ginger's nightclub acts and suffers a psychological disorder in which she believes she *is* Ginger. The Professor instructs the other Castaways to humor the "new Ginger" until he can straighten her out with hypnotism.

Meantime, Gilligan accidentally succumbs to the Professor's hypnosis and thinks he is Mary Ann. Mary Ann has altered all of Ginger's dresses and believes she really is the movie star until she is asked to sing a number onstage and she falls on the wooden stage floor, konking her head once more.

Note: In many episodes in which we had to sing, Dawn's voice was dubbed because, well, Dawn just couldn't carry a tune. Even when we all had to sing "For He's a Jolly Good Fellow," the director had Dawn mouth the words; otherwise, she would have knocked the rest of us off-key. Dawn was aware she was not Carole King, so she laughed about it. In *this* episode, however, some strained notes were needed to make Mary Ann's Ginger sound off, so Dawn just sang normally. W: Don Friedman, D: Steve Binder.

93. THE SECRET OF GILLIGAN'S ISLAND (DS) Skipper and Gilligan stumble upon prehistoric stone tablets in a cave and the Professor thinks the hieroglyphics etched on them may bring about their rescue. The rest of the Castaways search for the missing pieces of the tablets, and, finally, the pieces are nearly assembled—except the most important one. Gilligan has been using it as a serving tray, and when he drops it, the vital relic crumbles.

That night, Gilligan takes the Castaways back 3 million years in a dream in which he is a caveman chiseling on stone a secret way off the island. W: Bruce Howard (story by Bruce Howard and Arne Sultan), D: Gary Nelson.

94. SLAVE GIRL Kilani, a pretty slave girl, is eternally committed to Gilligan for saving her life. Everyone is jealous of Master Gilligan for having a personal servant, but he wants nothing to do with Kilani. Later, Gilligan must fight Ugandi, Kilani's ex-boyfriend, in a duel to the death. The Professor concocts a sleeping serum for Gilligan and the natives assume he has died but they insist on giving him a proper passing ceremony and burning the body.

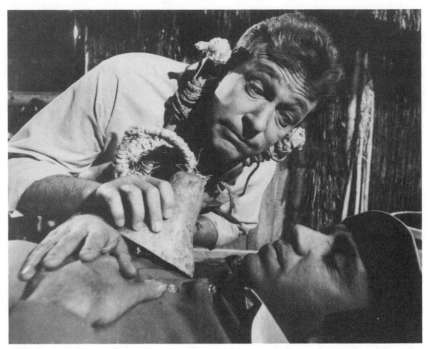

Checking Gilligan's pulse while he lay in a cataleptic trance to fool the natives in "Slave Girl." (© 1993 CBS, INC.)

Gilligan wakes up after the other Castaways fail to save him from the flames. W: Michael Fessier, D: Wilbur D'Arcy, GC: Midori (Kilani), Michael Forest (Ugandi), and Mike Reece and Bill Hart (natives).

95. IT'S A BIRD, IT'S A PLANE   An air force jetpack lost at sea finds its way to the island. The Professor runs a series of tests and believes it is filled with just enough fuel for Gilligan to fly back to Hawaii. Naturally, Gilligan ruins every attempt at a rescue. W: Sam Locke and Joel Rapp, D: Gary Nelson, GC: Walt Hazzard (Air Force lieutenant).

96. THE PIGEON   This episode is about a bird, but I think most people remember it more for the gargantuan spider.

Here's the Professor's rescue plan: Tie a note on Walter, the homing pigeon that Gilligan has befriended. The only problem is that it will take two weeks to build up Walter's strength for the journey. The others are so impatient they force-feed him until he's bloated. Now it will take another two weeks for Walter to diet and get in shape.

Meanwhile, we see the pigeon's owner, a prisoner on the mainland named Burt (nicknamed "Burty" or maybe "Birdie") who cares for a whole cage of birds like Burt Lancaster in *Birdman of Alcatraz*. When Burty receives the constant pleas for help attached to his pigeon, he responds in disbelief.

When the bird flies back to the island, it becomes endangered in a cave that houses a deadly six-foot black morning spider, which ends up trapping all the men in the cave with the pigeon. Mrs. Howell rides a bamboo pushcart with a mirror attached into the cave in an attempt to scare the spider with its own image. Finally, the pigeon attacks the spider and kills it. (We never learn what happened to the spider's corpse. Maybe the Castaways pushed it off the cliff.) Finally, when the pigeon is sent back with yet another plea, Burty believes it's from ol' Mrs. Hawkins and is never convinced that it's real.

Note: The giant spider was first seen on "Lost in Space." Our stunt man, Janos Prohaska, was inside the spider manning the legs as it crawled along. W: Story by Jack Raymond and Joel Hammil and teleplay by Brad Radnitz, D: Michael J. Kane, GC: Sterling Holloway (Burt), Harry Swoger (prison guard).

Character actor Sterling Holloway (the original voice of Winnie the Pooh) played a prisoner with a fascination for birds in one of our last episodes. (COURTESY OF SHERWOOD SCHWARTZ).

97. BANG! BANG! BANG!   A crate of newly developed thermo-plastic explosive putty has been lost at sea, and the government is worried that the pliable material might get into the wrong hands.

The container washes ashore, and the Professor identifies the molding plastic as thenaformaldehyde, which they can shape into combs, plates, nails, and other useful objects. The Professor even fills Gilligan's cavities with the substance, not knowing it could kill his patient.

Gilligan's monkey realizes that hurling the objects into the air causes them to explode on impact, and he showers the Castaways with random bombings, which nearly kill Gilligan. W: Leonard Goldstein, D: Charles Norton, GC: Rudy LaRusso (Michaels), Bart-lett Robinson (Hartley), Kirk Duncan (Parsons).

98. GILLIGAN, THE GODDESS   King Killiwani searches the island for a White Goddess who will marry a volcano and be a sacrifice to it. Saving the women from such a fate, the men try out for White Goddess, and Gilligan wins. King Killiwani falls for "Gil-liana," the new White Goddess in high heels, only Gilligan can't stand the charade and removes his dress and wig.

King Killiwani think White Goddess evil, take henchmen, and leave island (sic). W: Jack Paritz and Bob Rodgers; D: Gary Nelson; GC: Stanley Adams (King Killiwani), Mickey Morton and Robert Swimmer (the natives).

Skipper as the White Goddess? We didn't know it, but this was our last episode ("Gilligan, the Goddess"). (© 1993 CBS, INC.)